Charles Dickens in middle age

Dickens
IN HIS TIME

IVOR BROWN

THOMAS NELSON AND SONS LTD
LONDON

THOMAS NELSON AND SONS LTD
Parkside Works Edinburgh 9
36 Park Street London W1
117 Latrobe Street Melbourne C1

THOMAS NELSON AND SONS (AFRICA) (Pty) LTD
P.O. Box 9881 Johannesburg

THOMAS NELSON AND SONS (CANADA) LTD
91–93 Wellington Street West Toronto 1

THOMAS NELSON AND SONS
18 East 41st Street New York 17, N.Y.

SOCIÉTÉ FRANÇAISE D'ÉDITIONS NELSON
97 rue Monge Paris 5

Printed in Great Britain by
Thomas Nelson (Printers) Ltd, London and Edinburgh

CONTENTS

ILLUSTRATIONS

All the illustrations are reproduced by kind permission of the Radio Times Hulton Picture Library.

We thank the following for their kind permission to quote copyright material.

A. & C. Black Ltd for a quotation from VICTORIAN COMFORT by John Gloag

Paul Hamlyn, Publishers for a quotation from LONDON LABOUR AND THE LONDON POOR by Henry Mayhew

Oxford University Press for quotations from PORTRAIT OF AN AGE by G. M. Young and THE DICKENS WORLD by Humphrey House

Thames & Hudson Ltd for a quotation from CHARLES DICKENS, A PICTORIAL BIOGRAPHY by J. B. Priestley

CHAPTER ONE

World and Writer

WHEN Charles Dickens was born in Portsmouth in 1812 there were only sailing-ships in the harbour. When he was taken to live in London two years later the journey had to be made by road, at the best pace that a horse could manage. It was the road down which Nicholas Nickleby and Smike walked wearily until picked up by Mr Crummles driving that unprogressive pony described as 'good at bottom, if not elsewhere', descended from the finest circus talent, and 'quite one of us' in the Crummles theatrical company.

The *Doughless*, a three-masted sailing ship

The Navy which Dicken's father was serving in the Pay Office on shore was not essentially different in equipment from that which had defeated the Spanish Armada. But the age of steam transport at sea immediately arrived. In 1812 there was a passenger service launched on the Clyde. Not only the Scots but the Americans were ahead of the English on the water, for steamboats were plying on the Hudson river between New York and Albany in 1807. The first English naval craft to use steam took the water at Deptford in 1823. It was called *Lightning*.

In 1814 coals were hauled by steam along an iron track at a colliery, but much of the underground haulage continued for several decades to be done by children whose condition was nearly that of slavery. However, the Age of Speed was arriving and in 1825 the passengers from Stockton to Darlington in the north could go by train. Speed was something which Dickens never liked but had to accept and could later on profitably use in the saving of time. Radical in politics, he was conservative in travel, and up to his death in 1870 he liked to welcome his guests at Gad's Hill near Rochester in Kent with an old-fashioned drive in a horse-drawn coach of the kind he had loved in his boyhood.

He lived his early life in a world where distance had meaning. Our triumph, if triumph for mankind it be, has been to abolish distance. By express train, motor car, aeroplane, and rocket the increase of speed and expansion of range have been carried to such fantastic lengths that there is nothing left, not even the moon, that can be called 'over the hills and far away'. The outer space of the earth is circled in the time that Dickens took to cover a few miles. It is not a victory in which he would have gloried, for his first thoughts were always with the effect of change on human beings and he was contemptuous of statistics. The achievements of machinery impressed him as little as the figures and facts of the economists and statisticians which he loved to ridicule. Had he lived in the epoch of the astronauts he might have pointed out in his usual incisive way that the new masters of space had not mastered the simple problem of putting up enough roofs to provide reasonable living room for their people and that there was little advantage in exploring a barren planet before we have so cultivated our own earth as to make famine everywhere unthinkable.

The year 1812 was momentous abroad. The Duke of Wellington led his armies to hard-fought victories in Spain, and Napoleon, with his cause sinking there, began his disastrous march into Russia. The English no longer feared an invasion or looked to their rustic Home Guard of 'Fencibles' to help the regulars if 'Boney' came. Britannia, whose name Dickens liked to use in mockery of a too complacent nation, was now, with her chief dangers past, serviceably ruling the waves, but not so surely that she could sweep to victory in the futile war with America begun in 1812. The country gentlemen of England could sally out from the serene classic porticos of their country houses to hunt and to shoot animals and birds, not Frenchmen, while their ladies entertained in their charming Regency dresses and suggested a trip to Bath, where was much gossiping and revelling as well as use of the curative waters.

Wars, for the civilian inhabitants of an unmolested island, were rather like football matches played away. The results were heard and discussed, but they were decently remote and the news came long after the event. For the combatants, fighting with sword and bayonet as well as with bullets and cannon-balls, there were savage struggles and the carnage, with no proper medical services, was appalling. But such sufferings were unshared. The London of the Prince Regent was, in its wealthy quarters, a scene of elegance, gaiety, and debauchery. Even when the Napoleonic War was at a desperate crisis, before Waterloo, there were music and dancing for the officers and their ladies at a luxurious gathering in Brussels. On

For the combatants, there were savage struggles

15 June 1815, as Thackeray told the readers of his *Vanity Fair*, 'the talk and interest of the ladies regarding the ball was much greater even than in respect of the enemy in their front'.

Except in the new steam-powered factories, away in the midlands and the north and out of sight of the notables in London and the squires in the country, it was a static world and had been for centuries. History, 'the crimes, follies, and blunders of mankind', repeated itself not only with the same sins and sufferings but also with the same technique of waste and destruction.

These wars, in which the rough and dangerous work was mainly done by poor men, who were strangely meek since they had nothing whatever to gain from them, had been incessantly conducted by their rulers to satisfy personal ambition or greed for new and wider possessions. But until the European use of gunpowder began in the fourteenth century they had been fought with weapons which had remained the same for some thousands of years. What Shakespeare called 'this villainous saltpetre' and conservative soldiers of the sword regarded as a sordid and contemptible way of killing was after its introduction used for a very long time in a very elementary way. Compared with the monstrous inventions of our own time progress in the craft of slaughter, if progress is a word that can be applied to such a matter, had hardly moved at all.

From the beginnings of man's life until the nineteenth century movement and communication were limited by the speed of a sailing-boat or of a rowed galley at sea and of the human foot and some beasts of burden on land. When an Ancient Greek philosopher travelled in his country or through the islands of the Aegean Sea in the fifth or fourth century B.C. he made his journey in the same way as the English Dr Johnson, who went by horse from London to Scotland and then sailed among the Hebrides in A.D. 1773. In 1844 Charles Dickens took his family across France to Italy and to do so bought an old and capacious horse-drawn coach, thus travelling no faster than a Roman officer or governor going from Britain or Gaul back to his capital.

Something like a thousand years passed between the composition of Homer's *Iliad* in Greek and the continuation of that saga by the Roman poet Virgil, who used the same form of metrical verse as Homer before him. Virgil's Rome was conquering and dominating the whole known world from Britain to western Asia, but it did so with the weapons used by Hector and Achilles around the walls of Troy. The Romans understood organisation and lawgiving but their amenities and luxuries were no improvement on the elegance, comfort, and sanitation achieved by the inhabitants of the isle of Crete in 1500 B.C. Nor was the life lived by the English gentry in the eighteenth century an advance in material comfort on the standards reached by the Cretans; in some ways it was less civilised since the Cretans had developed the craft of sanitation in a way that Europe was to forget to a deplorable degree. Dr Johnson, and even Dickens in the following century, had worse plumbing than King Minos of Crete. Things of this kind were expected to go on without going forward, at any rate in steady-paced England. There was neither hope nor fear of great differences to come in the fabric of human society.

Christianity overcame the pagan religions in Europe, but the wars and the struggle for domination did not cease. Slavery continued in the exploitation by the Christians of the coloured races. The new religion had savage sectarian wars of its own. Material conditions, whether in the luxury of the few or the poverty of the many, altered very little. For centuries Christianity, while seeking to save and purify souls, paid scant attention, even in its holiest cities, to health, cleanliness, and sustenance of bodies. There were occasional revolts and revolutions of the exasperated masses, but they were either bloodily put down or led to a new lust for conquest, as in the wars which followed the French Revolution. In these the revolutionary ideas of human brotherhood and liberty were forgotten amid the march of armies which could move no faster than those of Julius Caesar.

This constancy in many of the conditions of life was naturally reflected in the matter and methods of authorship. During the time which elapsed between the age of Homer and the birth of Dickens the writers of poetry, plays, and the stories which came to be called novels were not, and could not be, aware of the chance of sudden and drastic alterations in the social scene. Their world had a fixity which has vanished from ours. They had their feet on firm ground. Story-tellers entertained with their fables and inventions, first by reciting and then by writing. They drew on the past to 'tell sad stories of the death of kings' and made their tragedies for the actors out of conflicts long ago. The lyric poets sang of love and beauty and wine and laughter. Single persons might be selected for mockery in comedies which made fun of their oddities or pretentions. The artists were engaged in criticising this or that form of folly, but they were not seeking to reform in any radical way the entire social structure. Even the most liberal-minded Greeks thought slavery a natural state for defeated or barbaric people, who could rightly be used as 'living tools'.

For three thousand years the story-teller had excited and amused, or at the highest level of his work examined human character in all its fortitude and frailty. But it was the character of the individual that was probed and portrayed by this kind of authorship in various grades of quality. Shakespeare, to take the summit of achievement in this kind, was masterly in his study of the single man or woman; he did not set out to be what we call a student of society or a clamorous reformer. During his lifetime of fifty-two years there was a dynastic change: Queen Elizabeth died and James VI of Scotland and I of England united the two crowns. Commerce expanded and the population of the country grew slightly larger, and most of it grew no richer since the possessors remained in possession and the value of money declined. The anger of Shakespeare, who could be very angry, was directed at the vices of the individual, greed, pride, lechery, cruelty, and so on. His age knew all about the Deadly Sins and did not arraign the Deadly Society as so many writers were to do, with Dickens at the head of them, in the nineteenth and twentieth centuries.

The story-teller, or novelist as we say now, did not conceive it to be his or her business to use words as dynamite for blowing up the social order. Jane Austen, who died when Dickens was a boy of five, took the English country gentleman's way of life for granted. Napoleon might storm across Europe; but paying calls and party-giving would go serenely on. During the eventful years between 1796, when she began to write *Pride and Prejudice*, and her death in 1817 she held her sensitive mirror up to the foibles of human nature as if there were no national or social problems. 'Problem' is now a word of which we read and hear daily and almost hourly. The air, as well as newsprint, is full of eager and anxious people explaining and discussing their problems. But problems were no concern of the novelist until Dickens, beginning with journalism, started to mix his fictions with the facts of public misery and injustice and to make his stories a reformer's challenge as well as a feast of entertainment.

Jane Austen

A notable example of the novelist withdrawn from political and economic observation and from critical survey of the great contemporary changes in the state of the nation was Sir Walter Scott. During his sixty-one years of life (1771-1832) the face of central Scotland was being rapidly enriched and befouled with the onrush of the new steam-powered industries, fed with the local coal. Glasgow, long a useful harbour and a western outlet for the sailing-ships, was Britain's pioneer in steam navigation and speedily became a thriving centre of the new industrialism. Population grew rapidly and workers swarmed to the mills and factories. New families arose with a new economic power far exceeding the sway of the old clan chieftains. What a world for an observant man to write about! But Sir Walter, working in his Tweedside home, which he furnished and decorated as a medieval museum, turned his back on this urgent and superb subject, using the English as well as the Scottish history of many centuries past to provide the backgrounds for his huge outpouring of romances. Only in *St Ronan's Well* did he bring his fictions up to date, and then he did not go to the Clyde: he stayed in a Border spa. The steamers on the Clyde, the new surge of mingled wealth and poverty, and the creation of a brash and ugly Scotland were not for him. He could respond to a riot in Edinburgh if it were a hundred years old and could be viewed as history. The 'pressing modern problem', if he saw it at all, was no concern of his.

But at the end of the eighteenth century the whole pace and strain of the common life were being intensified. The Industrial Revolution was properly so called. When steam-power set the wheels revolving it meant more wealth for some and less well-being for most. The crafts which had remained unchanged through the ages had a quality which machine production could not emulate. But quality ceased to count. The Age of Quantity had arrived, quantity of goods that were not so good, of money that multiplied itself by shrewd investment, and of crowds who flocked into the factory towns and bred plentifully amid the squalor. These towns were being built without plan or provision or scruples of any kind. The Age of Quantity was also the Age of Anyhow.

The poets had begun to notice these things. Being aware of human values and sensitive to human suffering as well as to the natural beauty which the Age of Anyhow was destroying they spoke out. Of course men and women of feeling had always been revolted by cruelty and had made protest in their prose or poetry, but they did not identify the common sufferings with the prevailing organisation of industry or of politics. When the ideas of the French Revolution began to spread some poets tended to be more direct in their protests. Wordsworth, who was later to be a steady conservative with his eye on the lakes and mountains and not on the new Lancashire that was making a smoky wilderness of bricks and chimneys so close to his paradise, had for a while welcomed the ferment of new ideas and thought it bliss to be alive in such a dawn. Shelley, who did not live to accept the Age of Quantity and Anyhow and certainly would never have accepted it had he lived to be seventy instead of dying at twenty-nine, gloried in the revolutionary spirit and was one of a group who believed that the methods of human government were the cause of human misery.

'Government,' Thomas Paine had written, 'even in its best state, is but a necessary evil; in its worst state, it is an intolerable one.' The circle of rebellious thinkers in which Shelley moved went further than that; they asserted that government was really not necessary at all, since man was naturally an innocent who could be trusted to behave himself if only he was released from the shackles of an imposed discipline. That 'poets are the unacknowledged legislators of the world' may seem an odd statement for Shelley to make, since he was devoted to poetry and as an anarchist distrusted or even loathed legislation. But his intended meaning is plain. Poets must be teachers, mixing counsel and even politics with their word-music. This is a complete contradiction of 'art for art's sake'. If the poet is to be our guide to good behaviour as citizens in a difficult world he cannot linger dreaming in an ivory tower or moralise only in a tranquil wilderness of lakes and mountains.

William Blake, a poet and a mystic of the same period, was also ready to have his eye on the framework of society. He said that he saw angels in his London garden; he also saw the Devil at work in the 'dark Satanic mills' of the new industrial England. He denounced the smoky chaos of factories, slums, and sweated labour which Dickens was to describe in the Black Country wanderings of little Nell in *The Old Curiosity Shop* and later in his picture of Mr Bounderby's Coketown in *Hard Times*. Blake was also sufficiently a student of politics to realise that dictatorship, whether on the far right or the far left wing of politics, was no remedy but only a corruption of the soul of a nation. He condensed his opinion in two stinging lines:

'The strongest poison ever known
Came from Caesar's laurel crown.

But while the men of vision were emerging as rebels, though not actually entering politics, the poets and dramatists still had their gaze fixed on the past or were averting it from the sweeping changes of the present. Dickens was to make an end of that.

Lord Byron did carry a protesting temper into the House of Lords and might have been a poet-politician had he stayed on in England. But his fashionable public wanted his biting wit and not his radical opinions and preferred the satirist to the rebel. He died for freedom in Greece when Dickens was a boy of twelve and had already seen the London of the workaday thousands in all its poverty, drudgery, and hunger as he worked in the dark and rat-ridden premises of Warren's Blacking Warehouse at Hungerford Stairs near Charing Cross. Dickens was not there very long, but the squalor and the misery remained with him in bitter memories all his life and did much to determine the form which his writing was to take. This was fiction based on facts, the facts of a suddenly changing England, where supremacy of the old families and their hangers-on was being shared with the new lords of money and machinery, while the poor remained the poor.

Dickens loved the theatre all his life. He very nearly became a professional actor and was accounted excellent in the amateur performances to which he gave quite a lot of his time and energy. But the drama of his time flourished on make-believe and did not tell the public about current realities, for which kind of truth there was no public demand. On its lighter side it provided long nights of mingled farce and melodrama, in which laughter and excitement were all that mattered. Plausibility of story or comment upon the way in which people really lived were the last things required. It was a theatre of escape, never intended to 'take people into themselves' as we say, but only to take them out of themselves into a tinsel world of gallant heroism, preposterous villainy, and beautiful heroines, or, on its comic side, of gay buffooning that set the house in a roar of laughter. On its serious side it had nothing to say of here and now; it looked to past ages and foreign scenes as much as Shakespeare had done in his day.

When Shelley wrote his play *The Cenci* his theme was sin and suffering in a long-vanished Italy, and Byron too, who was for a while intimately connected with the stage of his time as one of the directing committee at Drury Lane, turned to the chronicles of other countries for his subjects. It seemed to be an unwritten law that if a poet wrote for the theatre he should remove himself as far as possible from the world of his contemporaries and his neighbours. If Dickens had chosen to write for the serious side of the theatre in the early part of his career, either attempting poetry or using his prose, which in emotional passages sometimes tended to take the form of blank verse, he would probably have felt it his duty as a dramatist to fetch his plots out of the canals of Venice or from a palace in a bygone Rome. It was well that he did not waste his energy and genius in that way. He was a stage-struck man and he did have a hand with his friend Wilkie Collins in a romantic drama of the Far North called *The Frozen Deep*. But he was fiction-struck too and fortunately writing fiction became his chief way of life. In his journalism (and he kept finding time for that) he argued the case. As a novelist he gripped myriads who could not be bothered with argument and wanted a tale, not a thesis.

What Dickens did for the novel by making it a critical survey of his time as well as a gripping narrative was not done for the theatre until some time after his death. Ibsen in Norway had begun with the old romantic saga-subjects before he turned to realism and drove right into the heart of the contemporary community, whose shams he was determined to show up. Bernard Shaw, a boy just on fourteen when Dickens died in 1870, later expounded and championed Ibsen's attacks on the pillars and pretensions of society and carried on the work of exposure, using the stage as his platform for attacking the old and false ideas and ideals and proposing his remedies for the moral, economic, and political failures of the time. Shaw read Dickens closely and knew the novels in detail. The two men differed greatly in their temperaments and talents, but they had a similar approach to their work. Nowadays they would be called 'social realists'. When Shaw was told that the drama should not try to teach people the business of living sensibly and decently he curtly replied that it should do nothing else. Dickens, since he was born a brilliant story-teller, would not have gone so far as that, but he certainly regarded himself as a man with a message and a mission and not simply as a spinner of yarns.

As a boy he had been able to use the books which his usually impoverished father had sensibly collected; perhaps they were too tattered to be worth pawning. 'He was a terrible boy to read', said his nurse Mary Weller, a name which he was soon to immortalise. She described his habit of holding his book with his left hand while holding his wrist with his right, and constantly sliding it up and down while he sucked his tongue in a complete absorption. He had begun to read widely during his first schooling in Rochester, where he was happy enough, and continued later in

Camden Town and at Southwark, where he was not happy at all. The flights of fancy which relieved the fears and miseries caused by the family's hard times swept him into the East of the Arabian Nights, the island of Robinson Crusoe, and the Spain of Don Quixote.

The English scene was enlivened for him by the adventures of Fielding's Tom Jones and the rollicking, tumultuous fortunes and misfortunes of the very lively characters of Tobias Smollett. So he had been learning the story-teller's craft from a wide range of past masters. Much of his enjoyment had been of the narrative style called picaresque, a word of Spanish origin. Its dictionary definition limits it to the adventures of rogues, but it has been more generally applied to tales with no compact plot and describing a series of scattered incidents and chance acquaintances in a story of wanderings. Thus it was natural that Dickens's first novel, *The Pickwick Papers*, was of this kind. Here was, in his earliest venture into fiction, a panoramic survey in rich diversity of the humours of English life. There were the beginnings of his indignation at the nonsense of the politicians and the lawyers and at the cruel follies of the penal system; but it was its laughter that won him an immediate victory.

There was a drastic change of method in his next book, *Oliver Twist*. For this he created a complicated plot, and rather tiresome it is at times. But the essence of the tale is angry protest at the abominable treatment of paupers, especially of the workhouse child, and the filth and misery of the London slums which bred human as well as animal vermin and were the factories of manifold crime. There is some amusement of course but the ludicrous workhouse beadle, Mr Bumble, is not only a butt for comedy: he is a bully, a product of a Poor Law which needed to be exposed and overthrown. In the light-hearted theatrical and musical version of the story called *Oliver*, which proved immensely popular when produced in London

Ragged children in Lambeth in the early 90s

in 1960, Fagin, the criminal exploiter of a school of young thieves and a heartless scoundrel, was softened into an engaging old scamp and allowed to slide out of trouble. But Dickens had no such idea of the wretch and described him, without pity, on his way to the scaffold.

The novelist who was to scourge so many of the abuses and the malefactors of his age had suddenly emerged and immediately afterwards was to turn his lash on to the greedy and brutish owners of boys' schools, where unwanted children were deposited to rot in semi-starvation and often to die of cold, hunger, and neglect. As his work developed the whole tone and temper of the writing altered. The random pleasures provided by the picaresque novel were left behind and the serious purpose of purging and punishing the scandals of the national life determined the nature of these books and of the work to come. Great gusts of laughter, sometimes almost a hurricane of hilarity, were still to roar through the length and strength of the vast Dickens stories. But the laughter was the companion of the verbal lash. And the characters, instead of being fantastic, become more actual.

Sir Walter Scott died in 1832 at a time when Dickens was establishing himself as a speedy and accurate reporter in the gallery of the House of Commons. In 1833 Dickens saw the first of his essay-sketches in print and began to follow this up under the pen-name of Boz with graphic studies of London life, some of them grim portraits of its ugliest side. In 1836 a selection of these was successfully published in book form. The mainly jovial *Pickwick Papers* began to appear in serial form in the same year. *Oliver Twist* followed in 1838 and *Nicholas Nickleby* in 1839. A new kind of novel had been born, a novel no longer rooted in the romantic past, like Scott's, or withdrawn from nine-tenths of current happenings, like Jane Austen's, but relevant to the hard facts of hard times in all their light and darkness and offering its readers not just a solace for idle hours but a challenge to their sense of right and wrong.

CHAPTER TWO

The Politicians

POLITICS in our time have been so much bedevilled by international conflicts and threats of further conflict that foreign affairs have naturally been the chief concern of prime ministers, presidents, and dictators. During the lifetime of Dickens the Napoleonic and American Wars had ended in his early childhood and serious international crises were afterwards less frequent. There was the Crimean War in his middle period and later on the menacing rise of a bellicose Prussia. The scandalous mismanagement of the former evoked some of Dickens's sharpest ridicule at the expense of the placemen and muddlers in Whitehall. In this he was attacking a gross incompetence which existed under his nose in London. If European politics interested him at all he kept them mainly out of his novels and their leading personalities were scarcely known to him. He enjoyed travel in Italy and France but he went abroad for a rest or a change; there he was a social observer, not a student of statesmanship. Bernard Shaw, in an introduction which he wrote for an edition of *Great Expectations*, related that when the famous Italian Liberal Mazzini called on Dickens in London, the visitor's name was unknown and the visitor himself taken to be some foreign nuisance who wanted money and could be politely got rid of with a sovereign.

Home affairs, not foreign affairs, were the centre of his attention and the target of his onslaughts. And in home affairs homes themselves were a dominant theme, the wretched, overcrowded, insanitary homes of the poorest people. His mind was also gripped and his anger roused by the immense power that was being acquired

The wretched, overcrowded, insanitary homes of the poorest people

by the New Rich, who were encroaching on the once immense and still considerable power of the Old Rich. Into the City of London had come flagrantly dishonest adventurers, who promoted joint-stock companies and, when their schemes crashed, left the small investors ruined and the workers unemployed. These types were exposed in his early writing, in *Nicholas Nickleby* for example, and still more in his later books, especially in *Little Dorrit*.

During the middle of the century many financial speculations had gone up like rockets and come down like the sticks; but the chief gamblers did not fall alone. Thousands suffered with them. While *Little Dorrit* was being written the corpse of John Sadleir M.P., who represented an Irish constituency in Parliament, was found outside Jack Straw's Castle, a well-known inn on Hampstead

Heath, where Dickens himself liked to take a chop for his lunch after a walk or a ride. There was a poison bottle beside the dead man's side. A letter was left by Sadleir saying, 'I cannot live. I have ruined too many. I could not live and see their agony. . . . I blame no one, but attribute all to my infamous villainy.' In another letter he wrote, 'It was a sad day for all when I came to London. There are serious questions as to my interest in the Grand Junction and other undertakings. Much will be lost by the creditors if these cases are not fairly treated. The Grand Junction, the East Kent, and the Swiss Railways, the Rome Line, the Coal Company are all liable to be entirely lost now.' He poured out his regrets in a lavish style worthy of a Dickens character, but that did not help the investors. Sadleir had actually been a Junior Lord of the Treasury in the Government of Lord Aberdeen, who became Prime Minister in 1852. Despite that Sadleir had used a respected name to run wild-cat schemes in which the savings of many depositors in Irish banks as well as of many English investors in railway shares and other ventures vanished.

Shortly before Sadleir's suicide a Yorkshireman called George Hudson had been a powerful personality in the railway world, where, while the lines were being widely developed during the eighteen-forties, immense profits were first made and then rashly expected to continue and increase. But Hudson, known as 'The Railway King', toppled off that supposedly golden throne and was charged with fraud. So the character of Mr Merdle in *Little Dorrit* was drawn from two lives—and one death. For this Mr Merdle, whom all London regarded as a solid pillar of unshakable prosperity and on whose advice many hung while they sponged on his hospitality, was also made to topple and to take his own life in despair. Of Merdle's suicide Dickens wrote:

> Numbers of men in every profession and trade would be blighted by his insolvency; old people who had been in easy circumstances all their

> lives would have no place of repentance for their trust in him but the workhouse; legions of women and children would have their whole future desolated by the hand of this mighty scoundrel . . . the greatest Forger and the greatest thief that ever cheated the gallows.

The ghosts of Hudson and Sadleir walk in the last half of *Little Dorrit*, where Merdle 'the recipient of more acknowledgement within some ten or fifteen years than had been bestowed upon all peaceful public benefactors and upon all the leaders of the Arts and Sciences' ends by cutting his own throat.

The public should not have been so easily gulled but the period was one of vast hopes. Huge early gains had led to the later and fatal confidence. It was the new age of share-worship. There had been great expectations and great collapses before. The South Sea Bubble was more than a hundred and thirty years away when Sadleir's body was found on Hampstead Heath. But the fortunes to be made out of the new factories and especially out of the new railways created further and abounding faith in investment. In *Our Mutual Friend* Dickens scornfully described the new idolatry:

> Have no antecedents, no established character, no cultivation, no ideas, no manners; have Shares. Have Shares enough to be on Boards of Directors in capital letters, oscillate on mysterious business between London and Paris, and be great. Where does he come from? Shares. Where is he going to? Shares. What are his tastes? Shares. Has he any principles? Shares. What squeezes him into Parliament? Shares.

In the mood of his last work finance was politics for Dickens. But throughout he had thought as much about poverty as about opulence, haunted by the abominable social conditions in which splendour and squalor were close and contrasted neighbours. He was convinced that it was penury that created crime in all its forms. It was a view long held by Radicals and Socialists, but we can

A pitiful kind of escape, the gin-palace

hardly be so confident now when it is discovered that in our Welfare State and so-called Age of Affluence and Opportunity, with employment at reasonable wages far more general than it used to be, the figures of crime and especially of violent crime keep rising in a menacing way. The men who have coshed a bank-cashier or a jeweller and got away with a load of cash or diamonds have not done it because they have no hope of a job or are hungry for bread.

However that may be, Dickens had to watch such poverty and hunger round about him that it was then natural to see in privation the source of robbery and assault. Slums, he insisted, were the breeding-grounds of the criminal, and the despairing effort to forget these hovels and tenements led to a pitiful kind of escape by way of the well-lit, well-warmed, alluring gin-palace. So politics for him were not the battle of the polling-booths, which he believed to be a sham fight. Nor was he much inclined to insist on the immediate and wide extension of the right to vote which other Radicals were demanding. He wanted clean air instead of fetid vapours in the streets and had only contempt for the hot air of oratory on the hustings and in the Houses of Parliament.

His way was to denounce the twaddle spoken by the more gaseous politicians and to show up the Parliamentary leaders as a gang of duffers who had only brains enough to see that their party-game was maintained with one or other of their cliques to control the play. They had their own technique for always managing to do the wrong thing—or nothing at all. Chapter 40 of *Bleak House* begins with an ironic outburst against the big political families, who really were so very small in their capacity.

> England has been in a dreadful state for some weeks. Lord Coodle would go out, Sir Thomas Doodle wouldn't come in, and there being nobody in Great Britain (to speak of) except Coodle and Doodle, there has been no Government. . . . But England has not appeared to care very much, but has gone on eating and drinking and marrying and giving in marriage, as in the old days before the flood. But Coodle knew the danger and Doodle knew the danger and all their followers and hangers-on had the clearest possible perception of the danger. At last Sir Thomas Doodle has not only condescended to come in, but has done it handsomely, bringing in with him all his nephews, all his male cousins, and all his brothers-in-law. So there is hope for the old ship yet.

Some may think that the Doodle and Coodle game has not yet been played out.

But sarcasm pulls down no slums and builds no homes for the people in their place. The reforms would have to come either by revolution, which Dickens dreaded and would never have assisted, or by measures carried through a reformed Parliament. In fact there were electoral reforms in his lifetime and some considerable social improvements, belated but salutary, insufficient but better than nothing, did come by way of Westminster. But Dickens was so contemptuous of Parliament and politicians that he was demanding a better world while despising and neglecting the means of getting it.

During four very impressionable years of his life, between the ages of twenty and twenty-four, he was a Parliamentary reporter. These were also four very important years in the history of Parliament. They included the electoral Reform Act of 1832, the Factory Act of 1833, and the abolition of slavery in British Colonies in 1834. In the same year came the Poor Law Amendment Act, which entirely altered though it did not at once improve, and in some ways made harsher, the treatment and relief of destitution. There was also the Municipal Corporations Act, which instituted elected Councils after a Commission of Inquiry had reported with justified severity on the bribery, peculation, and general inefficiency of the previous local rulers. These changes did not go far but at least they showed a break with the travesty of democracy which had hitherto existed, with the ruthless individualism which gave the workers no legal protection against abominable conditions, and with a local regimen which was a welter of muddle and corruption.

The Reform Bill of 1832 was only passed after outbreaks of popular violence. Nottingham Castle was destroyed by fire and there was arson too in Bristol, where the Mansion House and the Bishop's Palace were badly burned. The protests were occasioned by the action of an otherwise unteachable House of Lords in rejecting the Reform Bill, and the Lords were only scared into accepting the measure by the King's promise to create a sufficient number of peers willing to support it. Thus the possibility of more widespread rioting was averted, a fact which might well have impressed Dickens, who was later to show a strong fear of violent mobs and of the possibility of mob-rule arising from the chaos. At least the principle had been established that counting heads is better than breaking them.

Yet the electoral reforms thus gained were small. One hundred and forty-three constituencies out of six hundred and fifty-eight, those with tiny electorates, some of them actually having two members and known as Rotten Boroughs, were swept away and the seats redistributed. The chief extension of the vote was to all freemen in corporate towns and to 'ten-pound householders'. The county people were still voteless unless they paid a rent of fifty pounds a year, which excluded all of small or moderate means. The ten-pound householders did not include a large number of urban workers and the labourers on the land were completely excluded. The Radicals had every reason to be disappointed at the slenderness of that victory. But the House of Lords had been defeated and the rule of the aristocracy, who controlled the Rotten Boroughs, began to be replaced by the rule of the rapidly expanding commercial middle class. The reformed Parliament thus created was able to press on with legislation of a kind hitherto unthinkable and some advances were made by the Ten Hours Act of 1847 and the Public Health Act of 1848.

The number of voters was still very low. In 1867 only 900,000 out of 5,300,000 adult males had electoral rights. This was ended by Disraeli's measure of 1868, which enfranchised all rate-paying householders in the towns, lodgers paying a rent of ten pounds a year, and those living in the counties and having a rating qualification of twelve pounds a year. An amendment in favour of women's suffrage was moved by John Stuart Mill and seconded by John Bright, but rejected.

Electoral reform had again been backed by threatening public demonstrations and was denounced by its terrified opponents as a 'leap in the dark'. Two million new voters were thus created. But the countrymen had to wait until 1884 for the possession of equal rights with townsmen, and there were no votes for women until the Great War of 1914–18 had shown that a sex whose members could go anywhere and usefully do anything, in the Services as well as in the factories, could no longer be ranked with juveniles and imbeciles.

The discontent of the workers with the Reform Act of 1832 led to a vigorous political campaign for a complete democratic Charter. Its leaders were Lovett of the London Working Men's Association, who believed in legal and constitutional agitation, and Feargus O'Connor, who was prepared to advocate violence. The Charter which they put forward contained six demands: annual Parliaments, manhood suffrage, vote by ballot, equal electoral districts, payment of members of Parliament, and the abolition of the property qualification for Members. This was only a moderate programme of which four points were in time accepted. The claim for a Parliament of only one year's duration was unlikely to be popular and certainly would not be popular now, when the uncertainties, the expense to the candidates and parties, and the general nuisance of a General Election every year would be welcomed by very few. But it is obviously true that an elected majority may outlive its popularity rapidly and continue to govern in spite of that. Theoretically the Chartists had reason on their side, and the demand for equal electoral districts, also reasonable in principle, has been largely met by frequent redistribution of seats according to shifts in the population. But it has been deemed advisable to allot seats to isolated communities with special local interests, such as the inhabitants of the Northern and Western Isles of Scotland, although their electorates are well below that of all the urban constituencies and many county ones. That is a small point which the Chartists, had they seen it, would hardly have bothered to oppose.

There was nothing in these purely political proposals to put the fear of revolution into the moneyed and governing class. But the threats of violence did create a widespread alarm and the movement was much weakened by the disputes between the 'physical-force' wing, a voluble minority, and the more numerous advocates of peaceful persuasion.

The climax came with the announcement of a monster meeting to be held in London on Kennington Common. Troops were called out to maintain order and protect the citizens from possible riot and pillage. But during the eighteen-forties there had been

'The leaders urged them on to fearful cries and threats'
The Old Curiosity Shop

some significant social reforms passed by Parliament, conditions of labour had been slightly eased, and those malcontents whose Chartist zeal had been caused more by economic than by political grievances lost their enthusiasm. There was no battle of Kennington and Chartism, with its fervour quenched by reform without and by dissension within, faded away.

Dickens was intensely pacifist in his attitude to agitation and therefore the militant Chartists could get no support from him. He feared the mob enraged and in *The Old Curiosity Shop* (chapter 45) he had given a terrified and terrifying picture of a working-class upheaval in which 'maddened men, armed with sword and fire-brand, spurning the tears and prayers of women who would restrain them, rushed forth on errands of destruction to work no ruin so surely as their own'. This was the spectacle seen by Little Nell in the industrial midlands. By the apprehensive novelist the Black Country was imagined running with blood, plagued with mortal pestilence, and with its nights of anguish broken by the screams of orphans and distracted widows and 'the rumbling of rude coffins'. This vision of inferno was never realised, but evidently the thought of its possibility had given Dickens a shiver-some nightmare.

But it was not only these gruesome fears which made him no Chartist. A programme limited to bettering the membership and procedure of Parliament could be of little interest to one who was profoundly cynical about 'the talking-shop' and all its ways. Our knowledge of his life as a Parliamentary reporter is lacking in detail; we do not know what debates he covered in the extremely important years of his work in the writers' gallery. But we are left in no doubt as to his general attitude. He was utterly bored. In *American Notes* (chapter 8) he told his readers:

I have borne the House of Commons like a man, and have yielded to no weakness, but slumber, in the House of Lords. I have seen elections

> for borough and county, and have never been impelled (no matter which party won) to damage my hat by throwing it up into the air in triumph, or to crack my voice by shouting forth any reference to our Glorious Constitution, to the noble purity of our independent voters, or the unimpeachable integrity of our independent members.

He was asked to stand for Parliament and refused, not only because he said he could not afford it but also because he wished to maintain his personal freedom. It is well for us that he took this negative line, because had he given time to debating and passing Bills he would have written the less. Westminster's loss was a public gain. Though a fine speaker on the platform he might have lost his temper in the House and proved a tactless and therefore unhelpful supporter of the measures which he intended to back with all his strength.

About the conduct of elections and the choice of candidates he remained fiercely sarcastic. He had turned the Eatanswill election of *The Pickwick Papers* into a riotous farce and much later in *Our Mutual Friend* he wrote one of his most sardonic chapters on the entry to Parliament of the newly rich Mr Veneering. It is called 'A Piece of Work' and begins:

> Britannia, sitting meditating one fine day (perhaps in the attitude in which she is presented on the copper coinage), discovers all of a sudden that she wants Veneering in Parliament. It occurs to her that Veneering is a 'representative man'—which cannot in these times be doubted—and that Her Majesty's faithful Commons are incomplete without him. So Britannia mentions to a legal gentleman of her acquaintance that if Veneering will 'put down' five thousand pounds, he may write a couple of initial letters after his name at the extremely cheap rate of two thousand five hundred per letter. It is clearly understood between Britannia and the legal gentleman that nobody is to take up the five thousand pounds, but that being put down they will disappear by magical conjuration and enchantment. . . .

'Suppose there are two mobs?'
'Shout with the largest'—*The Pickwick Papers*

> Veneering then says to Mrs Veneering, 'We must work,' and throws himself into a Hansom cab. Mrs Veneering in the same moment relinquishes baby to Nurse; presses her aquiline hands upon her brow, to arrange the throbbing intellect within; orders out the carriage; and repeats in a distracted and devoted manner, compounded of Ophelia and any self-immolating female of antiquity you may prefer, 'We must work.'

So with a cry of 'We must work' Veneering and his friends dash round London. There is a general readiness 'to take cabs and go about'. The going about is fast and furious. Clubs are visited and the lobby of the House of Commons is canvassed by a couple of eager toadies called Boots and Brewer. 'We'll bring him in,' cry one and all. The money has been found. The independent electors of Pocket-Breaches are approached. Veneering says that he is coming among them as a mariner returns to the home of his childhood, 'a phrase which is none the worse for his never having been near the place in his life and not even now distinctly knowing where it is'. He is 'brought in'.

So much for representation. G. K. Chesterton wisely pointed out that Dickens was sadly impressed by the difference between popular government and representative government. The former he wanted, yet believed to be almost unattainable, if not impossible. Representatives, in his opinion, were not chosen but foisted on to the voters and when elected behaved in a quite unrepresentative way. This view he summed up in a speech made at Birmingham less than a year before his death: 'My faith in the people governing is, on the whole, infinitesimal; my faith in the People governed is, on the whole, illimitable.' He amplified this later and explained that while the hearts of the People (he stressed the capital P) are sound, the heads of the people who govern the People are not. Parliament was thus continually frustrated even in its good intentions, hopes of reform proved chimerical, and lawgivers turned out to be the obstructers of society instead of its helpers.

This continuing pessimism and his own consequent isolation from politics can well be criticised as barren. Hopes of reform had not all been proved false and so keen a student and historian of Victorian society as G. M. Young dismissed the completely cynical opinions of Dickens about politics as nonsensical. The censurers of this negative attitude could say that Dickens was really an impractical railer, and there is something in that. He idealised the People while he was afraid of their gullible stupidity. He was nervous of mass-action, but politics inevitably means appeal to the mass and handling of the mass. He was saying to the People, 'You are fine fellows and you could have a fine time if only the rich would stop fleecing you and the lawyers would stop tying you in the fetters of antiquated laws. But really that can't be done, so you will have to go on as you are, fine but frustrated. Your votes, if you have them, get you nowhere and if every man, woman, and child had a vote you would still be nowhere.' To which a puzzled member of the People might well have replied, 'If we can't get our rights peaceably with our votes, why are you so indignant and so frightened if we suggest getting them forcibly with our fists?'

In the introduction to *Great Expectations* already mentioned, Bernard Shaw reasonably maintained that Dickens was a revolutionary without knowing or facing that reality. Karl Marx was Dicken's contemporary in London, studying and analysing and condemning to perdition the same bourgeois society run by the Coodles and Doodles and alternately enriched and ruined by the Merdles. The exposure of British political ineptitude, administrative jobbery, and financial robbery in *Little Dorrit* made that book in Shaw's opinion even more seditious than Marx's *Das Kapital*. He described it as genuine dynamite compared with the Marxian red pepper. But the governing people whom Dickens ridiculed were too conceited to recognise their own portraits and too complacent to be worried about what they thought was a novelist's fun.

Marx, in his logical way, demonstrated that domination by such nincompoops as the Dickensian Coodles and Doodles, with the ubiquitous Tite Barnacles at their side, could only be overthrown by a dictatorship of the proletariat. What Marx did not see was that a mass cannot be a master without being mastered and that a dictatorship of the proletariat is an illusory idea. What must happen in times of violent revolution is a dictatorship of one or a few strong, resolute, and clever men, probably not proletarians themselves (Lenin was the son of a senior civil servant and went to Kazan University), over the proletariat, who will have to be even more drastically regimented and dictated to by the new régime than ever they were by the old. With the aid of modern weapons, which enable the few who possess them to hold down millions who do not, and of modern methods of propaganda and brain-washing by a strictly controlled press and radio, an able man can dictate to the proletariat, Dickens's idealised People, with devastating success. But that future world of mass-discipline and mass-doping was outside the range of Dickens's limited vision.

We cannot blame a master of fiction for not being an acute analyst of the social facts and a political seer. In *Little Dorrit* and elsewhere he had set down imperishably the Victorian scene as he saw and hated it. He could say that it was not his function as a novelist to provide the answers to the questions which he raised. Since he both despised and despaired of the democratic and constitutional methods of reform and would have nothing to do with revolution, he could not possibly be a doctor prescribing cures for a sick nation. Shaw summed up Dickens as 'an unphilosophical Radical with a complete disbelief in government by the people and an equally complete hostility to government in any other interest than theirs'. Abraham Lincoln had already uttered his memorable but misty phrase about 'government of the people by the people for the people' when Dickens made his Birmingham declaration about the People governed and the people governing. But, said Shaw, Dickens never called on the People to remedy their own abuses. 'He would as soon have thought of calling on them to write his own novels.'

A lawgiving body must have an executive to put the laws into practice. Behind Parliament is the Civil Service. Dickens had as much contempt for the second as the first. It has been pointed out that the atrocious confusion of the Medical Health Service and of the Supply Departments at the War Office during the Crimean War made the blundering in Whitehall conspicuous. But the composition and qualifications of the Civil Service officials had been questioned before that. It had been pointed out to Mr Gladstone, who was Chancellor of the Exchequer in 1853, that the Service was a nest of jobbery and nepotism, and he was responsible for a Commission of Inquiry which led to the important Northcote-Trevelyan Report issued later in that year. Gladstone must have seen for himself the shocking state of affairs. If he did not make his own discoveries he was privately enlightened by 'a leading reformer' in a private letter which survived and became public. It told him that 'the introduction of well-educated, active men' would force those already with desks in Whitehall to bestir themselves, an exercise which they would deeply resent. They would be angered if they could not get their own ill-educated sons appointed under a reformed system. 'The old-established political families', it was said, habitually batten on the public patronage—their sons legitimate and illegitimate, their relatives and dependents of every degree, are provided for by the score.'

This was the scandal at which Dickens hit out in his picture of the Tite Barnacles in *Little Dorrit* and of the Circumlocution Office, of which the Barnacles were permanent and powerful occupants. Here was the fortress of such characters as were cartooned seventy years later as Dilly and Dally; along with incompetence and delay was concealment. 'All the business of the country', Dickens wrote in his ridicule of the Barnacles, 'went through the Circumlocution Office, except the business which never came out of it; and its name was Legion.' This was not the only stronghold of the Barnacles. 'The Barnacles were a very high family and a very large family. They were dispersed all over the public offices and held all sorts of public places.' The chief Barnacle, who was at the head of the Circumlocution Office and told his Minister what to say in Parliament if 'some vagabond had been making a tilt at the Office in a newspaper', had not only put in his son but had married into the family of Stiltstalking, which brought them too into the bureaucracy.

There was also a Lord Decimus Tite Barnacle who had long been a leader in the great art of 'How Not To Do It' and in the oratory of the 'It behoves me' kind. It always behoved him to see that the enterprise and self-reliance of a free and mighty nation were not cramped by the pestilent efforts of interfering reformers. 'The discovery of this Behoving Machine was the discovery of the political perpetual motion. It never wore out, although it was always going round and round in all the State Departments.' The slow and needless passing on from one department to another for further minuting is a habit still criticised. The Tite Barnacles as a family may have been 'winkled out' of their crevices round Downing Street, but the verbose and cloudy style which Civil Servants use in their correspondence, documents, and innumerable forms, though officially deplored, remains. It is an obstinate linguistic limpet which can fairly be called 'the Barnacular'.

Improvement came slowly. Four years after Florence Nightingale had coped with the chaos created by the military Barnacles she was still complaining that the War Office was very slow, expensive, and incompetent and that the Minister's intentions could be frustated by the dilatory and mutually conflicting departments. The attacks of Carlyle as well as of Dickens, and indeed of all reformers aware of the Barnacle nuisance, prevailed only after a decade and a half, when appointments to the Civil Service had to be made on an examination basis. In 1870 Gladstone effectively abolished the patronage system and made room for 'the scholarship boys' whom the owners of a Barnacle mind continued to regard with suspicion and dislike. But the system worked and first-class brains were introduced to the Administrative Grade, thus providing a Civil Service which, though blamed for overcautious methods, was no longer made up of placemen and was not to be charged with corruption.

It could not be claimed that when Dickens was buried in Westminster Abbey the Coodles and Doodles had wholly disappeared from that neighbourhood. Nor could it be said that the practice of circumlocution disappeared for ever. But the sixth-form boys and later the sixth-form girls were chosen on scholastic merit in a fair and partly open field, a territory in which the Tite Barnacle Doodles had no chance of surviving. The field was by no means wholly open because the 'People' were still outside this newly widened governing class. The way to the higher ranks in the Civil Service had to be taken mainly, if not entirely, by those whose parents could send them to costly schools and universities where scholarships, if won, would pay only a part of the educational cost. But the new system, though not yet democratic, brought the universities much closer to public life and created an aristocracy of intellect in the place of the old 'boobocracy' amid which a few families, such as the Dickensian Tite Barnacles, had been living their quiet, lazy, useless, and obstructive lives.

CHAPTER THREE

The Worker

IT IS hard to believe that during the first year of Dickens's life some of the conditions of the Elizabethan economy were not yet extinct. That was true, at least in theory, of the worker's wage. We are accustomed to think of the Tudor period as one of intense and active individualism; but that was not the case in its attitude to the treatment and rewards of labour. The idea of a 'just price' for work or commodities had survived from the Middle Ages and in the sixteenth century wages were not simply a matter for bargaining between an employer, who might be powerful, and a worker, who was probably defenceless, so that the latter had to take anything he could get. The idea of a common responsibility for morally fair dealing had survived and by the Statute of Artificers the magistrates had the power to regulate wages and conditions of apprenticeship with an eye to justice. In principle the master was not entirely master in his own house or workshop and the Statute could be a safeguard for the hard-pressed labourer if it were properly administered. This is not to say that the principle was also the practice.

It had long ceased to be so at the beginning of the nineteenth century. The average magistrate was not an unbiased administrator of medieval laws, and the Statute, though it had lingered on unrepealed, was finally abolished in 1813. Legally as well as in practice there were now no restraints on wage-bargaining; the notion of a 'just price' had completely vanished. The dominant gospel was that of free trade in the labour market and the worker had to shift for himself. The medieval conception of moral obligations in industry had been wholly supplanted by the acceptance of hard economic laws. But this supposed freedom did not include liberty to join trade unions for common protection. These had been forbidden by Pitt's measure of 1800 which made such combinations illegal. It is true that combinations of employers were also forbidden, but the passing of an Act does not mean the immediate execution of its orders. The employers evaded the regulations. It was emphasised in the previous chapter that legislation requires a competent and conscientious executive to enforce it, and this did not exist in the Britain of the Tite Barnacles in Whitehall and of judges and magistrates all over the country, who were often grossly partisan in their administration of the law and its edicts.

The French Revolution had brought high hopes to Radical thinkers and idealistic poets, but its effect on the British workers was depressing and even disastrous since it created panic among the wealthy and the powerful. Fear of 'red ruin and the breaking up of laws' stimulated reactionary measures, and though the Napoleonic wars increased employment they were followed by severe economic depression and drastic repression of the workers despite their protests and efforts to defend themselves. Moreover, the dominant philosophy and economic doctrines of the time were intensely individualistic. It was believed that freedom of contract was essential to the national prosperity, and it was argued that it was idle for the wage-earner to be in conflict with the masters since the interests of employers and employed were identical. It might have seemed obvious that a penniless and hungry man is not free except in name. He must work for what terms he can immediately get, whereas the factory-owner with money in hand can afford to wait until the worker is starved into taking any terms offered to him. With the right to combine forbidden by law the worker at the end of the Napoleonic Wars was scarcely more free than a slave, and children were actually sold in some industries into which they were driven.

The boy Dickens, as the son of a minor Civil Servant living in Kent the life of the less prosperous but by no means wretched or destitute middle class, could hardly then be aware of how other people existed. He was himself driven at the age of twelve into a warehouse in London, where he was as much a wage-slave as any of the proletarians and could see for himself the common lot. In the year in which he was thus miserably employed the Combination Acts were repealed owing to Radical pressure. But that Dickens was aware of his new right to join a trade union was obviously most unlikely and in any case the trade union was not there to join. It took many years to build up even the beginnings of the powerful trade-union structure that we know today.

Such development had to come by stages. That going too fast might be a mistake was shown in the life of Robert Owen, a Welsh idealist who first had a cotton-mill in Manchester and then started a model factory at New Lanark in Scotland. He was an early Socialist who rebelled against the ruling creeds of capitalism and individualism; but he inevitably roused the enmity of other em-

Charles Dickens at the blacking warehouse. 'No words can express the agony of my soul.'

ployers and his enemies exploited his religious scepticism as well as his new-fangled Socialism to discredit him.

Owen helped to form in 1833 what he hoped would be a monstrous power in the land, a Grand National Consolidated Trades Union with political as well as industrial objectives. Seeking to include so much, it was too cumbrous and too ambitious to succeed at a time when organisation of the workers was in its infancy and had a frightening sound in the ears of the general public. Trade unionism had to rise by stages and by separate units in separate trades and crafts. Combination had been legalised in principle but persecution continued in fact. In 1834, for example, six farm labourers of Tolpuddle in Dorset were convicted and transported to Australia for their humble and innocent trade-union activities. A case against those who might think they were combining lawfully could be faked up by charging them with some additional offence. The Tolpuddle Martyrs, as they came to be called, were accused of conspiracy in restraint of trade and of administering illegal oaths. The injustice and severity of their condemnation and sentence were so flagrant that a widespread agitation won their pardon and release two years later.

Politically Chartism dwindled away. Industrially the Grand National Consolidated Trades Union proved to be neither national in its appeal to the workers nor solid in its powers of endurance. But soon a more modest creation of unions limited to special occupations began to bring better results; a notable example was the Amalgamated Society of Engineers, founded in 1851. These unions were also friendly societies which attracted members by their benefit schemes. Their appeal was to the skilled and better-paid (or less ill-paid) workers, who could afford to pay fairly high contributions. The unskilled and poorest remained mostly unorganised. There was a fruitful development in co-operative shopkeeping begun at Rochdale in Lancashire. This enabled the co-operators to buy and sell goods for themselves and to keep the profits in the form of dividends on purchases. In time the 'Co-op' became a popular working-class institution, especially in the north of England. The repeal of the Combination Acts in 1824 had not brought to trade unions a sufficient and effective legal protection, but this was better guaranteed by an Act of 1871 and confirmed by subsequent measures.

In *Hard Times*, written in 1854, Dickens had two main subjects in a book which is less than half the usual length and has a look of scrappiness, as though the author had a sense of failure and was glad to be done with it. One of these themes was close to his heart; that was the inhumanity of the economists, who reduced living people, chiefly the poor people, to rows of figures, and would allow no place amid all this arithmetic to feeling or to fancy. Everything must be factual, tabulated, argued out in terms of statistics to prove that the workers were there to work and that the more money they made for others, the more, but very little more, would accrue to them in the very long run. Much earlier, in *The Chimes*, Dickens had created the character of Mr Filer, the acute statistician who could prove that 'a description of animal food commonly known to the labouring population of this country as tripe, is without exception the least economical and the most wasteful article of consumption that the markets of this country can by possibility produce. The loss upon a pound of tripe has been found to be, in the boiling, seven-eighths of a fifth more than the loss upon a pound of any other animal substance whatever.' To Mr Filer, with his slide-rule applied to edible paunches, *Hard Times* added Mr Gradgrind, whose name has taken a permanent place in the English language as a synonym for thrifty calculation and resolute application of economic law to everything, from the conduct of a shop or a cotton-mill to the control of the human heart and its affections.

'Tall chimneys out of which interminable serpents of smoke trailed themselves and never got uncoiled'—*Hard Times*

Beside Gradgrind is Josiah Bounderby, the self-made and all-powerful boss of industrial Coketown, a character who goes to such extremes of vanity, greed, vulgarity, and ruthlessness that some have regarded him as one of Dickens's failures, impossibly over-drawn, an ogre, not a person. This criticism is not certainly justified. Dickens had gone to Lancashire to observe the process of an industrial conflict in Preston, the Coketown of the story. He drew the Coketown scene directly from what he saw, the foul outpouring of smoke amid the gaunt imprisoning mills and factories, 'the black canal and the river that ran purple with ill-smelling dye and vast piles of building full of windows where the piston of the steam-engine worked monotonously up and down like the head of an elephant in a state of melancholy madness'. The people were alike, the streets were alike, the work done and the long hours kept were alike. The chapels of eighteen religious persuasions were alike, pious warehouses of the red brick which had everywhere become grimy and black brick.

The town was as much a piece of fact as the factual-minded economists of the Gradgrind school could desire. Amid the clanking machines men and women were themselves machines, weaving money for Bounderby. In creating the macabre image of Coketown Dickens was at his best, angry, graphic, and confident in his condemnations. He was not exaggerating the results of the Industrial Revolution in a North Country town, dependent mainly on one form of manufacture and ruled by one motive. So when he came to indict the bounce and brutality of Bounderby he may likewise have been drawing on reality, having met in person qualities as odious, or very nearly as odious, as those of Coketown's self-satisfied dictator. It is easier to say that Dickens was caricaturing a brash Victorian employer than to prove it. It was a hard world and full of hard-faced men. It is true that the early Dickens inflated the absurdity of his more amusing characters with the fanciful and fantastic gaiety of his genius for comedy. But by the time he had applied himself to Coketown and its problems he had changed to a more serious as well as sombre analysis of human society and to more realistic portraiture. He was no longer roaring with laughter; he was roaring with anger, and the wrath was based on the facts, facts, facts on which Gradgrind was feeding his bleak mind to the full. But Dickens reached very different conclusions. The author of *Hard Times* was quite capable of showing balance when he came to describe and investigate the workers' response to their sufferings and the upthrust of trade unionism.

The exposure by Dickens of the deplorable conditions in Coketown and similar caverns of drudgery amid the steam and smoke, an exposure adding still darker colours to the landscape of the

Black Country as painted in *The Old Curiosity Shop*, may suggest that he would be writing about Labour as a convinced class warrior on the workers' side and as an ardent champion of trade unions militant. In general sympathy he was keenly their supporter. Stephen Blackpool, the hero of *Hard Times*, to use a term now suspected as a relic of old-fashioned sentiment but fairly applicable in this instance, is a man with the traditional hero's heart of gold, carrying, along with the normal hardships of a Coketown mill-hand, his own personal burden of a miserable marriage to a woman who has become a hopeless drunkard. He bears his fate with heroic fortitude. His fellow workers, as Dickens describes them, are men of warm hearts and generous feelings, but they are turned against Stephen by the agitator Slackbridge when Stephen refuses 'to go along with them' in trade unionism and strike action. The reasons for that abstention are not properly explained in the story. We are given only the picture of a lonely, independent, isolated, and admirable figure, better able to express simple feelings than to argue his case. Stephen remains enigmatic, a handicap to the story. But it is significant and surprising that Dickens has chosen for his hero a man who will not be a trade unionist.

There is no mercy shown for the agitator. Slackbridge's style of oratory is as repulsive as that of the ranting and unctuous 'shepherds' of the chapels, whom Dickens loathed and lampooned. 'Oh my friends and fellow sufferers!' cries this fellow, although as a paid trade union organiser he is not suffering at all. He storms on about 'the holy and eternal privileges of brotherhood' while ready to make Stephen's life intolerable. It might be Pastor Stiggins in one of his alcoholic oozings of piety. Slackbridge carries the day and Stephen is driven out of all Coketown fellowship and sent to Coventry, although instinctively the workers know that he is a man of courage and integrity.

Here we meet the same division in Dickens's mind that was

discovered in his treatment of politics. He sees the workers, like the voters, as sound in moral essence but stupid and untrustworthy when policy is needed and as simpletons easily exploited. 'The people governing' the unions are as untrustworthy as 'the people governing' in Parliament. Further, trade unionism means action by the mass, and Dickens, so strong a believer in the merits of the alone-standing man, was fearful of men when massed. His individualism was mirrored in that of Stephen Blackpool. Another constant fear at the back of his mind was that of the mass not only massive but violent and ferocious. Some of the earliest trade unionism had threatened forcible methods, but the extremists were not strong enough to give grounds for any serious apprehensions. The fires of Chartism had burned down when *Hard Times* was written, quenched in part by the advocacy of physical force by some of its adherents. But Dickens would have none of that, and just as he cried for political reforms while despairing of and deriding the Parliamentary means necessary to achieve them peacefully, so he supported the Coketown workers' claims against the greed of Bounderby and yet made the hero of his tale one who would not 'go with them' in adopting the quite reasonable methods of trade-union action and in using the only weapon available to them without recourse to riot, the withdrawal of their labour.

When Dickens described in articles and used in his story the stoppage at Preston the workers had gained a ten-hour day, which seems long enough to us but was an enormous advance on previous conditions, whose harshness now seems almost incredible. When Dickens was twenty-one and reporting debates the reformed Parliament passed Lord Althorp's Factory Act. This limited the working-hours of children and young persons and created a system of factory inspection by officials with the legal right to enter factories and to see what was going on. Hitherto inspection had been left to magistrates, who might be friends and relatives of the employers, and to clergymen, who, at a time when the Church was passive and conservative, were unlikely to have much influence with the Bounderby type of manufacturer or mill-owner.

The firmly held belief of the economists that all state interference was dangerous and even damnable worked naturally to assist the employers in so long defeating any check upon the working-hours of adult males. The devotees of Free Trade, when they defeated the Corn Laws and kept down the price of bread to the benefit of the British workers and chagrin of the British farmers, applied their doctrine to the price of labour as well as to the price of food. When the Ten Hours Bill was being debated some of the Liberals were against it. Stubbornly loyal to their gospel of *laissez faire* and averse to all public interference in trade, men whose names stand high in the annals of Liberalism, Richard Cobden and John Bright, were in opposition, but such Liberal peers as Lords Russell, Palmerston, and Macaulay supported the measure. The Conservatives were also divided. Sir Robert Peel, who had been convinced by the failure of the harvest in 1845 that the Corn Laws, so precious to the Conservative rural interests, must go, was for the Ten Hours Act. For freedom of trade in one direction, he was for state intervention in another.

They were not all Coodles and Doodles in the Houses of Parliament and none did more for the causes that Dickens championed than the Earl of Shaftesbury, who made piety practical and translated Christian doctrine into Christian policies. It was he who said when Dickens died, 'God gave him a general retainer against all suffering and oppression', and he could justly have said the same of himself. Entering the House of Commons at the age of twenty-five and moving in 1851 to the Lords through the inheritance of his title, he made reform his passion and in many fields his accomplishment. The Poor Law, the treatment of lunatics and juvenile offenders, conditions in factories, education, and housing were all subjects for which he not only focused public attention, which was not so difficult, but also obtained redress of evils and the provision of definite action. This was much harder since there were so many ready to obstruct, some because of economic theories, others through selfish motives. Shaftesbury was untiring in his support of the Ten Hours Bill, and his work for a Lodging House Act, a housing reform long overdue, was praised by Dickens as providing one of the most useful laws that ever came out of Parliament.

The Poor Law and the treatment of paupers figure so largely in the novels and also in the indignation of Dickens that some picture must be given of its operations and alterations during his lifetime. During the wars following the French Revolution prices rose while wages did not and there was danger of undernourishment rising to starvation of the labourers, not least in the countryside. There was talk of fixing a minimum wage and to this the farmers were opposed. But something had to be done to prevent famine and the risk of rebellion. The magistrates of Berkshire met at Speenhamland near Newbury in 1795 to arrange and enforce a minimum wage, but they were diverted to a measure, afterwards known as the Speenhamland system, whereby the worker, instead of being paid adequately by his employer, drew a dole from the rates proportionate to any rise in the price of bread. Competition of local mines and factories had averted extremely low wages in the north, but in the south the dole was widely granted. This meant that the public was subsidising at its own cost the paying of starvation wages. It was a disastrous arrangement, except for the farmers and employers, and was soon proving a ruinous burden to the nation. It had to go. But it was ill replaced by the new Poor Law of 1834.

To the hungry and destitute who were deprived of the outdoor relief from rates which 'Speenhamland' had given them there was available the new type of workhouse, and it was decided that conditions therein must be more severe than those of paid, or

A workhouse, pre-1849

underpaid, employment in the factories or on the land. Hence the paupers' diet was fixed at the lowest level which could be expected to keep the inmates alive. Their feeding was not only meagre: it was shockingly unhealthy since in most places it allowed for no fruit or vegetables except potatoes. When the workhouse boy, Oliver Twist, made his famous request for more, he was only pleading for a second bowl of gruel, which is defined as 'a light liquid food made by boiling oatmeal or another farinaceous substance in water or milk'. It was made plain by Dickens that the Board of Guardians presiding over Oliver's workhouse were members of the plain-water school. They were not there to spoil the children with milk.

According to the account in the novel the children were 'issued three meals of thin gruel a day with an onion twice a week and half a roll on Sunday. . . . The system was rather expensive at first, in consequence of the increase in the undertaker's bill and the necessity of taking in the clothes of all the paupers which fluttered loosely on their wasted, shrunken forms after a week or two's gruel'. *Oliver Twist* is a work of fiction as well as an indictment of the Poor Law and we need not accept all its details as strictly accurate, but there is documentary proof that the No. 1 Dietary authorised by Poor Law Commissioners in 1836 included a pint and a half of gruel a day and said nothing of milk, tea, butter, fruit, or vegetables. Five ounces of cooked meat were allowed on three days a week and replaced by soup and cheese on three more. The meatless Fridays had suet or rice pudding for their speciality; the vice was in the monotony of starch. Some of the quantities are large enough. The portion of suet pudding was a pound in weight and may have felt like that when eaten.

There was more in the new Poor Law than Dickens admitted. It superseded relief by single parishes and set up larger and better-organised administrative unions. As Sir George Trevelyan pointed out in *English Social History* it created a central machine which by displacing the old local autonomy was used as years went by to remedy the grievances of the poor. Trevelyan decided that, while this Poor Law was harshly and incompetently worked at first, it had been intellectually honest within its limits and contained the seeds of its own reform. That grotesque bully, Bumble the Beadle, was a survival from the previous Poor Law, which was out of date when *Oliver Twist* was written. But Acts of Parliament are not immediately implemented everywhere in our own time and certainly were not instantly enforced then. Bumble is not necessarily a figure of fiction. That type knows how to hold on to a job; what he had been he could still callously remain for some time to come.

Dickens saved Oliver from apprenticeship to a grim specimen of the chimney-sweeping trade called Gamfield, whose very aspect was a new terror to an already terrified child. This escape was due to the mislaying of a magistrate's ink-pot when the indenture was to be signed. Oliver was handed over instead to Mr Sowerberry the undertaker for the sum of five pounds and was set to work among the coffins instead of the flues. He was thus rescued from one of the worst of all the fates which awaited the unwanted pauper child when the Poor Law sold him out of the workhouse; it was certainly not quite the worst, since had the scene of Mr Bumble's command been in the north of England the boy might have gone to the coal-mines. What he had been spared by going among the corpses and coffins was the existence of 'a climbing boy' with filthy and narrow chimneys as his workshop. It is surprising that Dickens did not send Oliver to that form of bondage since such a dispatch would have given him a range of savage cruelties to expose, and that he would have done with devastating power. He had another destiny for his derelict waif, preferring to make Fagin's school for juvenile thieves the principal academy in the education of the boy.

The workhouse children were thus disposed of by apprenticeship, which was a kind word for selling into slavery. Sometimes they were the victims of the Poor Law, sometimes of brutish parents who were glad to be rid of a brat deemed burdensome if they could pocket a few pounds in the process. A deal with a master-sweep was a common way to this piece of salesmanship. The usual age for the start on a new life was six or seven; sometimes it was even earlier. The mites were first taught to follow a senior boy up the chimneys; the smaller the novice the better, since the chimneys were often extremely narrow. What was tactfully called 'repugnance' to this training, in other words natural panic at the prospect of the dirt, the darkness, and the danger of a fall or suffocation, was cured by digging pins under the learners' feet or even by

A climbing boy

lighting a fire under them. They suffered from severe sores and cankers caused by continual rubbing against the chimney-walls and they became deformed by the ceaseless twisting and squirming on their way up. They were inevitably covered in soot and only at rare intervals were they bathed and scrubbed.

This vile exploitation of 'the climbing boys' continued from the eighteenth century right through the lifetime of Dickens. There were enough humane people to raise protests but there was a completely callous majority able to see that the protests were unavailing. Bills were introduced into Parliament whose provisions would mitigate the scandal; the idea of ending it altogether was long thought impossibly Utopian. Societies 'to supersede climbing boys' with machinery were hopefully formed, but the 'experts' explained that this machinery would never work and that only boys could penetrate the curves and crevices of the chimneys. In 1804 a Bill for the reform, not the abolition, of the system did pass through the House of Commons, but it was thrown out in the Upper House by a handful of lords, who included one archbishop and five bishops.

The arguments used to perpetuate the climbing were ludicrous. One defence was that many of the boys were illegitimate sons of the gentry, the assumption being that the crime of being a bastard and a nuisance justified any maltreatment. A noble lord pleaded that reform should be left to the moral sense of a nation which was 'the most moral on the face of the earth'. A dry comment on this came from Mr and Mrs J. L. Hammond, in whose book, *The Town Labourer, 1760–1832*, 'the shameful record of this slavery' is told with documented detail. They pointed out that this extremely moral Britain was the only country where such cruelty was practised.

During the reign of Queen Victoria there were further attempts to make illegal this type of apprenticeship, but the Acts of 1840 and 1864 were made ineffective by the contrivance of the master-sweeps and by the owners of great houses, since it was in their mansions that the chimneys were most difficult to clean. Even the magistrates connived at evasion. At last, five years after the death of Dickens, Lord Shaftesbury succeeded in getting an Act passed which ended an iniquity, to whose public comprehension and shame Charles Kingsley had usefully contributed with his book, *Water Babies*, published in 1863.

The children who were apprenticed to the coal-mines had a no less terrible life ahead of them. Had there been a Kentish coal-field in Dickens's time he might have had much to say about that, but as it was, the aspect of the industry which attracted his attention locally was the distributive side, especially the coal trade on the river Medway. He saw the pits on his midland and northern journeys but he never devoted a book to them as he did to the mills of his Coketown. Had he done so he would have had plenty of material for anger and expostulation.

In 1842 a Commission of Inquiry into the Employment of Children and Young Persons, for whose appointment Lord Shaftesbury had been responsible, as was usual in the case of so many good deeds in those years, revealed the facts. Children were sent down the coal-mines from the age of five with heavy jobs as fillers and pushers of trucks. As in the chimneys, the smaller were the more useful if the passages to and from the coal-face were very low. As time went on there were more rails for the trucks and the pushing and pulling were a little eased. But the heat and damp were merciless and the hours of work incredibly long, ranging from twelve to sixteen in the day. Girls as well as boys were sent down the pits, and the Report described them at work: 'Chained, belted, harnessed like dogs in a go-cart, black, saturated with wet, and more than half-naked, crawling upon their hands and knees, and dragging their heavy loads behind them, they present an appearance indescribably disgusting and unnatural.' It is surprising that any survived this kind of childhood, in which the prolonged and exhausting work was accompanied by physical cruelties if there was any slacking off or falling asleep. It was considered a notable reform when thanks to Lord Shaftesbury's measure of 1842 female labour underground was forbidden and the early age-limit for the employment of boys was fixed. It was fixed, unbelievably to us, at ten.

A child's life was no better in the mills and factories. In 1819 an Act was passed which put an age-limit of nine on the children who could be legally employed in the cotton-mills and a limit also on the daily hours of work for those between nine and sixteen. These were over thirteen in all, twelve of actual work and one and a half off for breakfast and dinner. The Hammonds point out that this was in fact no safeguard. Enforcement without adequate vigilance by qualified inspectors was found to be impossible. Inspection was carried out, if at all, by amateurs, the local magistrates, and clergymen, and a Bounderby would know how to cope with them. During the eighteen-forties there began a series of belated checks on the hours of work and a gradual extension of factory legislation, but Dickens did not live to see anything like the controls

Visit of a Government Factory Inspector to young girl workers, 1881

that were necessary and have since been achieved. The educational opportunities and terms of employment of young people today are criticised for their insufficiency. To Dickens they would have seemed generous beyond dreaming.

'Sweated labour', a term of which we happily hear much less nowadays, continued for a long time in the garment trade. Bernard

Shaw introduced a scene set in an East End 'sweat-shop' in *The Millionairess*, a play which he wrote in 1936. The wages mentioned there are twopence halfpenny an hour and a woman calls this 'a regular and proper wage', adding that when she was a girl she earned five shillings a week in a match factory. There are women in the Dickens world who work extremely hard with their needles and are bitterly poor, but their plight was not the worst of all in that period.

Protests came steadily from social workers and writers. William Blake in his *Songs of Innocence* had reminded the world of 'the climbing boy' thrown on to the market:

> When my mother died I was very young
> And my father sold me while yet my tongue
> Could scarcely cry 'Weep! Weep! Weep! Weep!'
> So your chimneys I sweep, and in soot I sleep.

'The Song of the Shirt', by Thomas Hood, published anonymously in *Punch* in 1843, made a big impact upon public feeling but the shirt-makers continued in drudgery and poverty,

> Sewing at once, with a double thread,
> A shroud as well as a shirt.

Hood's cry,

> Oh God! that bread should be so dear
> And flesh and blood so cheap!

had its echo on the children's behalf in another poem which drove at the conscience of the public. In 1844 Elizabeth Barrett, who married Robert Browning two years later, had stirred similar compassion, at least among those who read poetry, with 'The Cry of the Children':

For all day we drag our burden tiring
Through the coal-dark underground;
Or all day we drive the wheels of iron
In the factories, round and round.

Iron is not an exemplary rhyme for tiring and the merit of the poem was in its sentiments, not its composition. But the sincerity of indignation swept its lines into the hearts of many middle-class Victorians. They were reminded that there were still children being forced up the hazardous flues of the rich houses and that boys of ten could still be sent down the mines. Dickens's Coketown was to be indicted ten years later and its Gradgrind, we may take it, did not read poetry. It would have been as criminal a waste of print and paper to him as was the consumption of tripe to Mr Filer.

There are contented workers, happy in poverty and occasionally prospering, in this Dickens world. They are the individual craftsmen and owners of their shops or businesses. It may be as grim a trade as that of articulating dead bodies, with skeletons in the cupboard, as practised by Mr Venus, or the laying out and boxing of corpses not acquired by Mr Venus. Who happier than Mr Mould the undertaker, with his professional pride in the ample perfection of his mutes and mourning, not to mention his domestic pride in his plump daughters and his mixing of a drink? Solomon Gills, the maker of nautical instruments, has pleasure in his work even while his finances are depressed, and for him there is also the convivial company of the invincible Captain Cuttle. Joe Gargery is not a blacksmith in a large way, but he could have been as happy in his home as at his forge had he not married a wife. Even in one of the big, new, noisy industries, which Dickens did not like, that of the railways, Mr Toodle enjoys promotion on the engine's footplate. The coachman with a coach of his own to manage has his pride of position as well as his taverns. To be a person and not a unit was the joy of these men as their creator saw them. And those satisfactions are as real and plentiful as the sufferings in Coketown.

Continually we are impressed by Dickens's dread and loathing of size. Fat men could be genial and a joke; but human society must keep its tonnage down. He was repelled by the constricting and assimilating forces in human society. Man massed was for him man demoralised. Had he lived to see an achievement of wealth better spread and of full employment for adults with no enslavement of children, he would have welcomed the justice done to the worker but he would have detested most of the work. The monstrous London of today, every year so greedily devouring his own Kent as well as the other Home Counties that the town will soon reach from Reading to Southend and St Albans to Brighton, would have left him aghast and despairing. What would David Copperfield, who after work found the walk through the fields to Highgate so freshening and agreeable, have thought of a compulsion to queue outside a tube station in order to fight for a place among milling crowds in a suffocating, overcrowded train? And what would have been Dickens's opinion of the life of the myriads who spend two hours or more every day on suburban travel of that torturing kind in order to work in a vast cubic office pile in which a thousand typewriters click? He could not have endured the spectacle of men who are less and less their own masters and more and more the servants of gigantic combines. Ours is a London far more sanitary, with the drunken, dirty doctors and the sluttish, wheezy Mrs Gamps decently asphyxiated long ago in a drench of antiseptics. More sanitary, but is it more sane?

CHAPTER FOUR

The Prison-House

FIVE years before Dickens was born William Wordsworth had published his 'Ode on the Intimations of Immortality' in which he described how

> Shades of the prison-house begin to close
> Upon the growing Boy.

The poet's gaol was symbolic, a supposed confinement of the spirit. Upon Dickens the material presence of prisons closed early. While still a growing boy he made his way past the walls of the Marshalsea to his daily and detested work at the blacking factory near Charing Cross, a drudgery which was itself to him a shameful incarceration. When he went there he was just twelve years old, an age at which memories can become indelible and suffering can be acute. He felt that he had been 'abandoned' (his own word for the dispatch to work caused by his family's desperate poverty), and then only a fortnight later his father was arrested for a forty-pound debt and sent to the Marshalsea.

Charles was first lodged in Camden Town with a Mrs Roylance, generally supposed to have been the prototype of Mrs Pipchin in *Dombey and Son*. Later, to obtain an easier walk to and from the factory, he was lodged with kindlier folk in Lant Street, Southwark, one of the relics of Dickensian London which is not much changed. He was nearer to his work and nearer to the prison, nearer in fact to several prisons. Southwark was swarming with insolvency. Aptly was Bob Sawyer, that gay accumulator of unpaid bills, given his 'digs' in Lant Street.

The George Inn, Borough

If any street in London can claim to be the stamping-ground of literary ghosts it is surely the High Street of Southwark, 'the Borough', as it was called. Chaucer had written:

> Bifil that in that seson on a day,
> In Southwerk at the Tabard as I lay,
> Redy to wenden on my pilgrymage
> To Caunterbury with ful devout corage,
> At nyght were come into that hostelrye
> Wel nyne-and-twenty in a compaignye,
> Of sondry folk, by aventure y-falle
> In felaweshipe, and pilgrimes were they alle.

The Tabard whence the Canterbury pilgrims set out was badly

burned in 1676 and rebuilt as a coaching-inn with a yard. It was finally demolished in 1875 and replaced by a modern building in the style of the time. If Dickens did not know Chaucer's Tabard he saw the relics of 'a genuine antique' in the same place and with the same name. Close to it was the old White Hart where Mr Pickwick met Sam Weller. This was much altered in 1865 and pulled down in 1889. Half of the galleried George Inn remains close by, still much as Dickens must have known it. To Southwark on the Bankside had come the Elizabethan players. Shakespeare lodged there and his Globe Theatre, as well as the Bear-garden and other playhouses, was just to the west of the High Street. Two months in the Marshalsea is mentioned in his *Henry VIII* as a cure for disorderly conduct or failure to prevent it. In the early nineteenth century the region had Dickens himself in its streets and Leigh Hunt was a compulsory, imprisoned resident for two years. It is an illustrious haunting.

Southwark was a nest of inns because at one time London Bridge was closed at night. The City did not want all kinds of incomers, including Falstaff's thieving 'minions of the moon', arriving nocturnally when the Watch, scanty and incompetent, was least capable of dealing with trouble-makers. So the ordinary travellers who rode or drove into London from the south were compelled, if night had fallen, to put up there until the following morning, which made innkeeping prosperous. Why gaols abounded also may be due to the opinion of the City Fathers that criminals were better across the water. They had plenty of these already in Newgate and the Fleet prisons on their own side of the river.

The Southwark houses of correction were the Marshalsea, the King's Bench, and Horsemonger Lane. The Marshalsea was in existence in 1381 when Wat Tyler's insurgents from the country attacked it. Ben Johnson was sent there for his part in a duel which had a lethal result. It was used for the imprisoning and burning of

Protestant martyrs during the reign of Queen Mary. The poet George Wither, who wrote of love charmingly but unprofitably, was imprisoned there for debt in 1613, and it drew verses from an anonymous poet in the eighteenth century who found it

> Dismal as wormwood or repenting rues.
> Thither the graduates in sin resort
> And take degrees becoming Satan's court,
> There are instructed in the Paths of Vice,
> There sell good Linen, there they purchase Lice.

It was several times rebuilt and the form of it to which John Dickens was sent was constructed in 1811. It was closed in 1842. There is much said of it in *Little Dorrit* but the Marshalsea had gone when this book was written in 1855. This novel is expressly back-dated and begins in Marseilles, also with 'a villainous prison', in 1825.

The second of the Southwark prisons, the King's Bench, was also there for the young Dickens to view with disgust since it was not abolished until 1880. It had had many distinguished inmates, including Smollett, the novelist, gaoled for libel, and John Wilkes, the journalist agitator and M.P., also for libel. Benjamin Haydon, the painter who was constantly in debt, was in the gaol for that reason when Dickens was lodging as a boy in Lant Street. His Micawber had experience of the place for the same reason. It was a large establishment with two hundred and twenty-four rooms and not all the debtors were harshly treated. If they had any small money in hand or were given some by a friend they could buy their liberty for a day or several days. For a larger sum they had the freedom of the prison's 'liberties', an area which extended for some miles.

Leigh Hunt was sent to the third Southwark prison in Horsemonger Lane. Since Harold Skimpole, with his cheerfully vague ideas about money and his readiness to borrow from anybody, is accepted as a portrait of Hunt one would expect him to have been gaoled for debt. His offence, however, was libel on the Prince Regent, whom he had called in *The Examiner* a corpulent Adonis and 'a violator of his word, a libertine head over ears in debt and disgrace, a despiser of domestic ties, the companion of gamblers and demi-reps, a man who has just closed half a century without one single claim on the gratitude of his country or the respect of posterity'. That was frank if not false and consequent incarceration of the most severe kind might seem likely to us. But Hunt was allowed to furnish and decorate his room in a very elegant style and sat among his flowers, his piano, and his bookcases to receive his visitors, among them Charles Lamb, who likened this ample and civilised cell to a fragment of fairyland. But the Horsemonger, which remained till 1879, included in its population prisoners of all kinds, even murderers. In 1849 Mr and Mrs Manning were executed outside that gaol as a public spectacle for the murder of their lodger.

Dickens had some early and strong objections to capital punishment but later withdrew them. He hated above all things cruelty, and murder is undeniably cruel. For bestial ruffianism he came to support a penalty which many now think bestial. Few thought so then. One does not gather from *Oliver Twist* that he objected to the hanging of Fagin as an accessory to the murder of Nancy and a shameless corrupter of youth, but he described with disgust the execution before a great multitude who, to fill the time before the horrid event, played cards, quarrelled, and joked. During the eighteen-forties he was against the death penalty. He was infuriated by Macaulay's remark in the House of Commons in 1846 that its opponents were afflicted by 'a kind of effeminate feeling', and he inquired in the *Daily News* whether there was 'anything especially manly and heroic in the advocacy of the gallows' and whether it was necessary to regard Mr Calcraft, the hangman, as 'one of the most manly characters now in existence'. He also maintained, as is still maintained, that comparative statistics showed that 'where capital punishments are diminished in number crimes so punishable diminish in number too'. His opinions hardened later on and for gross brutalities he also at last approved the brutality of flogging. He was a man who changed his mind as his feelings burned within him, but certainly for a while he was revolted by the death sentence.

Public executions were entirely detestable to him. That of the Mannings he himself watched, but not of course for pleasure. In order to expose and denounce the filthiness of such a spectacle he took a party who paid two guineas each for places on a roof overlooking the scaffold. This gave him the material for a description of the crowd and for writing a powerful letter to *The Times* on the degradation and brutality of the proceedings. The protest was unavailing and public executions continued for nearly twenty years more. Public hangings were at last abolished by law two years before his death and his campaigning must have had some part in the termination of this national disgrace. At least the Victorian spectacles of execution were not as repulsive as those in Shakespeare's time, when crowds gathered at Tyburn to see condemned wretches not only hanged but 'drawn', i.e. disembowelled, before they were actually dead. That hanging, though without this added bestiality, could continue as a public entertainment until 1868 is an astonishing reminder of the crudity and callousness of early Victorian as well as of Georgian London crowds.

Imprisonment for debt was one of Dickens's recurring themes. With Mr Pickwick's stay in the Fleet it took a fairly important place in his first novel and it had a very important one in *Little Dorrit* eighteen years later. It can be argued with some justice that Dickens was so enraged by the disgusting conditions in the debtors' gaols that he was unduly sympathetic to reckless borrowers and forgetful of the creditors who had lent and lost their money; not all lenders are heartless usurers and may make advances out of kindness, not cupidity. At the same time he was scathing about Skimpole's complacent notion that somebody 'could sign something or make over something or give some sort of undertaking or pledge or bond' so that he could continue his butterfly existence without working or worrying. Dickens was always viewing money as an enemy of humanity, and the City man, money-lending for money-getting, was several times portrayed with contempt and even venom.

We need not press the point of his partiality for the borrowers. The legal treatment of debt was so grotesque as to earn his attacks, since it was utterly callous to the penniless debtor and quite merciful to the man who had something in hand to pay for his own room and comforts in prison. It cannot be said that John Dickens was harshly treated. In any case he was only in the Marshalsea for three months, during which he had a regular income of six pounds a week to provide meals for himself, his wife, and his younger children, who had joined him. Charles came in from Lant Street to feed with them in the evenings. Yet there was no effort to cut off or diminish this income in order to satisfy the creditors. The death of John Dickens's mother brought a small legacy to her two sons, and the elder, William, immediately obtained John's discharge by paying what was due. If the mother had lived for some years John might have stayed on till he became, like Mr Dorrit, a father-figure in the Marshalsea and almost enjoying that position while idling his life away.

The debtors' prisons were shabby, dirty, and insanitary, but those who could rent their own room avoided the worst of the squalor. There were stenches and pests. In hot weather (and John Dickens was there in the summer months) 'the walls and ceilings were blackened with flies' for which, in Mr Dorrit's time,

Mrs Bangham, an ex-prisoner and now a prison charwoman, set traps of vinegar and sugar in gallipots, remarking, 'What between the burial ground, the grocer's, the waggon-stables, and the paunch trade the Marshalsea flies get very large. Perhaps they are sent us as a consolation, if we only know'd it.' These words of cheer were for Mrs Dorrit in her birth-pains, in which ordeal she was attended by Mrs Bangham as midwife and a doctor in for debt, both sipping plentiful brandy. Yet little Amy Dorrit and the mother implausibly survived.

Mr Pickwick went to the Fleet for refusing to pay damages to Mrs Bardell for a breach of promise of marriage, a verdict which he held to be completely unjustified. He had the money to meet his legally determined dues, but he was so indignant at the chicanery of the lawyers, Dodson and Fogg, and the injustice of the verdict that he preferred prison to surrender. The description of the procedure and conditions at the Fleet can be taken as more accurate than exaggerated. But Dickens could happily state in the introduction to a reprinted edition of *The Pickwick Papers* that 'legal reforms have pared the claws of Dodson and Fogg' and that 'the laws relating to imprisonment for debt are altered and the Fleet Prison is pulled down'. That demolition occurred in 1844 and the Memorial Hall occupies the site. The prison, known to be in existence in the twelfth century, had been built among ditches by the side of the river Fleet, which was already an open sewer and became the cause of a terrible epidemic in 1355. In Shakespeare's time there were complaints to Whitehall that the Fleet was a stinking and dangerous nuisance. But many distinguished people were sent to the gaol upon its banks for various offences and survived, including William Herbert, Earl of Pembroke, one of 'the noble and incomparable brethren' to whom the First Folio of Shakespeare's plays was dedicated. His punishment was for seducing (or being seduced by) Mary Fitton, one of Queen Elizabeth's maids of honour and possibly the Dark Lady of Shakespeare's sonnets. Another famous inmate, and at the same time, was John Donne, later Dean of St Paul's, whose crime had been to marry without his father-in-law's consent. Mr Pickwick followed distinguished company to this insanitary pile, which, quite as much as the Marshalsea, merited the description, 'Dismal as wormwood or repenting rue' and the attribution of abounding lice.

Mr Pickwick was first introduced by a turnkey, Mr Roker, to a revolting room. This he was to share with a group, one of whom, in the words of Roker, 'takes his twelve pints of ale a day, and never leaves off smoking even at his meals'. Obviously here was a debtor with some cash in hand. This caused Mr Pickwick to remark to Sam Weller, 'It strikes me, Sam, that imprisonment for debt is scarcely any punishment at all . . . you see how these fellows drink, and smoke, and roar. It's quite impossible that they can mind it much.' Sam agreed as to some of the fellows. '*They* don't mind it; it's a regular holiday to them—all porter and skittles.' But he stressed the sufferings of the others, 'them as vould pay if they could and gets low by being boxed up . . . them as is always a-idlin' in public-houses it don't damage at all, and them as is alvays a-workin' wen they can it damages too much. "Its unekal," as my father used to say wen his grog wor'nt made half-and-half.'

Unequal indeed it was. Mr Pickwick would probably have been driven mad or died if he had remained 'chumming', in Roker's phrase, with the filthy, noisy, and drunken types with whom he was first placed. But as soon as it was discovered that he could pay for solitude Roker immediately offered him 'a capital room' in the coffee-room flight for a pound a week; here, for another seven and sixpence a week, a carpet, six chairs, a table, a sofa bedstead, a tea-kettle, and other small articles of use and comfort were provided. Company could be received. A hot port negus was available as well as beer by the gallon at 'the tap'.

Spirits were theoretically banned, but there was a black market in what was known as 'the whistling shop', where rum and gin could be bought. This den the turnkeys were bribed to overlook.

To be a prison officer was a profitable job; presumably Roker collected and retained the rents of the 'capital' rooms. In the previous century a warden of the Fleet had sold his job for five thousand pounds, then a fortune for a man in that position. So for those who could pay their way and did not choose to pay their debts, the Fleet could be a tolerable boarding-house if they stayed in their seclusion and were not smitten by the common gaol-fever, which was another name for typhus. The illustration of Mr Pickwick's room by 'Phiz' shows a lofty and fair-sized apartment with a large window and bottles on the shelf. There was no obligation to do any work unless the prisoner wanted to earn some cash, and there were few chances of doing that.

So far so endurable, for the well-to-do. But the plight of the prisoners who had no money was desperate. There were no regular rations of food. When they had pawned almost all the clothing in which they had arrived they were left to beg and to starve. Dickens interrupted his narrative to describe the sufferings of this class and to arraign the abominable system which prevailed when he wrote *The Pickwick Papers*:

> The poor side of a debtor's prison is, as its name imports, that in which the most miserable and abject class of debtors are confined. A prisoner having declared upon the poor side, pays neither rent nor chummage. His fees upon entering and leaving the gaol are reduced in amount, and he becomes entitled to a share of some small quantities of food, to provide which, a few charitable persons have, from time to time, left trifling legacies in their wills. Most of our readers will remember that, until within a very few years past, there was a kind of iron cage in the wall of the Fleet Prison, within which was posted some man of hungry looks, who from time to time rattled a money-box, and exclaimed in

'There was a kind of iron cage . . .'—*The Pickwick Papers*

a mournful voice, 'Pray, remember the poor debtors; pray, remember the poor debtors.' The receipts of this box, when there were any, were divided among the poor prisoners; and the men on the poor side relieved each other in this degrading office.

Debtors, whether 'in the poor side' or able to hire a room, were spared solitary confinement in cells, a punishment which bears with particular severity on those who are used to living in crowded homes with plenty of companionship. (Pentonville was founded as 'a model prison' in 1842 with complete separation of prisoners in single cells, but this was a torment to many of those who were shut off.) The debtors could play various games. There was a rackets court of a kind at the Fleet and there was a skittle-alley in the Marshalsea. The former had its convivial 'tap' as well as the illicit 'whistling shop' and the latter its Snuggery, where the Collegians, as Mr Dorrit called his cronies among the long-established prisoners, could have their gatherings. Visitors could come in and out and family men could make a home there, cramped and shabby, but still a home. The turnkeys were not all greedy and corrupt and Bob in *Little Dorrit* appears as the Kind and not the Wicked Uncle of the Marshalsea. The dreadful and destructive feature was the lack of occupation. Those with small hope of a settlement made possible by some external stroke of fortune were left to decay in health and character. There was nothing to do and nothing to expect. In *The Pickwick Papers* Dickens painted the Fleet in the lurid colours proper to an inferno. In *Little Dorrit* the Marshalsea is a study in grey, a picture of drab humiliations and despairs. But the reforms were slowly coming.

The history of the punishment of felons convicted for criminal offences makes revolting reading. The records of Newgate, a gaol which lasted with various rebuildings from the twelfth century until 1902, were mostly a chronicle of cruelties savage almost beyond belief. They included such torture as pressing, the *peine forte et dure*, in which the prisoner was crushed with heavy weights in order to force a confession of guilt, which made the victims' goods seizable by the Crown. Yet many a prisoner withstood the ordeal in order not to deprive his relatives and heirs of his goods. That ended only sixty years before Dickens, as a young reporter, saw this gruesome dump, into which women and children as well as the toughest criminals were thrown. He left his judgment on it in the thirty-fifth *Sketch* by Boz. The boys were mainly pickpockets. He afterwards used this material for his picture of Fagin's victims and pupils, who were taught their cunning by a master-criminal. The lads whom he saw in Newgate horrified him. 'Fourteen such villainous little faces we never beheld. There was not one redeeming feature among them—not a glance of honesty—not a wink expressive of anything but the gallows and the hulks, in the whole collection. As to anything like shame or contrition, that was entirely out of the question.' But he ended by indicting society rather than the childish miscreants, whom he saw as 'the hopeless creatures of neglect'.

'The condemned felon, guilty and despairing'—Boz, *Newgate*

The women too he found to be products of bad homes in foul slums, downcast wretches with their better instincts withered beyond revival. 'Talk to them of parental solicitude, the happy days of childhood, and the merry games of infancy! Tell them of hunger and the streets, beggary and stripes, the gin shop, the station-house, and the pawn-broker's and they will understand you.' They slept on mats on the floor of their wards but they had sufficient food. The felons, unlike the debtors, did not have to beg for scraps and face starvation.

Among the men were many sentenced to death since there was still capital punishment for far more crimes than murder. When Dickens was starting to write there were two hundred and twenty capital offences. After the French Revolution the governing class who made the laws in a quite undemocratic England were terrified of mob violence and robbery and believed that ruthless application of the death penalty for even such offences as a theft of five shillings would be their best protection. In 1810 the liberal-minded Sir Samuel Romilly introduced a Bill which would abolish capital punishment for such minor offences, but it was defeated. The Lord Chief Justice, Lord Ellenborough, asserted in the House of Lords that public security could only be maintained by a widespread fear of the gallows.

But the supposed safeguards were breaking down because juries, appalled at the thought of blood on their hands resulting from a verdict of guilty in cases of larceny, were beginning to find offenders innocent. Thus the very severity of the law was defeating its own purpose of deterrence. To counteract this tendency and also to meet the growing demands for a less barbaric penal system, two laws of 1832 and 1833 abolished the death penalty for various forms of theft, and in 1837, just after the Boz *Sketches* and the serial publication of *The Pickwick Papers*, the number of capital offences was cut down to fifteen. In 1861 there was a further reduction to four, murder, treason, piracy with violence, and setting fire to ships of war and arsenals; the three last were not common.

When Dickens made his early survey of Newgate many of the twenty-five or thirty prisoners under sentence of death had not been guilty of serious crimes; their cases would go to a recorder for consideration, and by that time many sentences of hanging were remitted. As he put it, the condemned men whom he saw did not appear to be anxious. 'They had all been sentenced to death, it is true, and the Recorder's report had not been made, but we question whether there was a man among them, notwithstanding, who did not know that, although he had undergone the ceremony, it never was intended that his life should be sacrificed.' But there were still executions in plenty and with ghastly circumstances attending them. In the gloomy Newgate chapel the most conspicuous object in its little area below the lectern was the condemned pew. There, in Dickens's words,

> the wretched people who are singled out for death are placed on the Sunday preceding their execution in sight of all their fellow-prisoners

'The Hulk, like a wicked Noah's Ark'—*Great Expectations*

to join in the responses of their own burial service and warning their recent companions to take example by their fate. At one time—and at no distant period either—the coffins of the men about to be executed were placed in that pew, upon the seat by their side, during the whole service. It may seem incredible, but it is true.

The hulks have been mentioned and one of them looms up importantly on the misty river and is seen from the marshes in *Great Expectations*. The idea of using old naval ships as prisons arose when the war of American Independence and later the Napoleonic Wars made all ships precious and voyages transporting convicts to the Colonies risky. So prisoners liable to transportation were kept on the hulks safely anchored in the Thames, working fettered and under armed guard at dredging the stream and other forms of hard labour.

In the damp and rotting vessels there was inevitable pestilence, including cholera. These hulks had been thought of as a wartime utility but in 1841 there were three and a half thousand convicts confined in them, and thirteen years later there were some thirteen hundred. They were supplied with libraries in which the principal books for the prisoners' entertainment were Paley's *Moral Philosophy*, Sturm's *Reflections on the Works of God*, *The Rites and Worship of Jesus*, and, most aptly, *The Pursuit of Knowledge under Difficulties*. The magazine *Household Words*, edited by Dickens and containing much of his writing, was held by one chaplain as 'unsuitable for prisoners'. It might have been better described as most suitable for those who imprison.

The Fleet and the Marshalsea, even with all their denial of hope and their likelihood of a lifelong and futile imprisonment, had at least a kind of rough humanity in their administration. The old inmates were adult children in a play-pen, and if by some means a trickle of money reached them they could drink themselves into a lethargic torpor. Outside the prisons and coping with defaulters who had comparatively rich relations was that strange institution, the spunging-house. There is a lively picture of one of these in Thackeray's *Vanity Fair*. Colonel Crawley, the reckless gentleman who married Becky Sharp, being deep in debt, was arrested by the bailiff, Mr Moss, and taken to Mr Moss's 'mansion' in Cursitor Street. There was no hardship involved and the company could be called distinguished, including military gentlemen and young blades from the Inns of Court, who had parties every night and 'punished the champagne'. 'I've got a Doctor of Diwinity up-stairs,' said Mr Moss to the Colonel, 'five gents in the Coffee-room, and Mrs Moss has a tably-de-hoty at half-past five and a little cards and music afterwards, when we shall be glad to welcome you.'

It is true there were bars, of the metallic, not alcoholic, kind, round the courtyard, but there was no lack of creature comforts. The 'tably-de-hoty' was forthcoming (with 'a prime boiled leg of mutton and turnips'). When the Colonel was asked whether he would stand a bottle of champagne for the company he consented and the company drank his health. The Colonel addressed a letter to his wife asking her to settle his account with a money-lender, which she did. It is difficult to understand what became of the spunging-house population if the wives and relatives were not so forthcoming. But Mr Moss was not in the business for nothing and somehow this ludicrous system, with its cosy domestic Marshalsea where the corks popped, was made to work.

There is no comprehending the laws of England in the early nineteenth century. They were unspeakably inhuman to the felons and curiously kind to the rich spendthrift, whose family could be expected to rescue him. They created the utterly illogical process of imprisoning a poor debtor until he could pay and keeping him idle in a gaol with no opportunity for working and earning, thus ensuring that he could not pay. 'Unekal', as Mr Weller said, and also unintelligible.

CHAPTER FIVE

Plays and Players

AFTER so much description of darkness it is a relief to turn to a house lit up and its tenants the players. Some are born actors, some achieve acting, and some have acting thrust upon them. The last class are often unhappy. Belonging to a theatrical family with a famous name they feel that they must take the stage, even though it be against their secret inclination, and then sadly discover that they are not quite up to the parental standard and renown. There is a fourth class, of the actors who might become great but are deflected from entering so risky a profession. Dickens can be considered as one of the great deflected.

He was always fascinated by the theatre and in his youth very nearly became a professional player. He took lessons in acting, learned famous roles, and was proposing to take an audition at Covent Garden when two things turned him aside. One was a severe chill, which made attending the audition impossible, and the other was sudden promotion in his work as a Parliamentary reporter, in which, at the age of twenty, he was already marked out as excellent in speed and accuracy.

It was well for the English novel that this deflection occurred, though it is likely enough that, since Dickens was even more of a born writer than he was a born actor, he would have broken away from the stage to the desk after one of the disappointments and humiliations that even the supreme players have at some time to face. But the passion to be seen and heard as well as to be read had its outlet. He became an industrious amateur player, his most notable performance being as Bobadil, that swaggering soldier in

Ben Jonson's *Every Man in His Humour*; and later in his career, at the age of forty-five, he began dramatic recitals of his work with the impersonation of the characters of his novels, in which his power and vividness of performance held huge audiences on both sides of the Atlantic amazed and enthralled.

Charles Dickens as Captain Bobadil in *Every Man in His Humour*

In our own time that gifted actor and devoted Dickensian, Mr Emlyn Williams, has given us a remarkable picture of Dickens thus in action; it was a very brave thing to attempt, especially since the audience of today is much less responsive to a forthright emotional display than was the Victorian public. Mr Williams carried it off triumphantly. But he would be the first to admit that Dickens must have been more overwhelming in the passionate and melodramatic episodes. It was with these that the novelist drove his auditors and spectators into the depths of pity for the victims tormented by bullies and oppressors. It was also the exhaustion caused by these which helped to wear him out fatally before he was sixty.

The theatre of his youth was very different from our own. It was dominated by the actors, who starred either in botched-up versions of Shakespeare's plays or in pieces by contemporary authors which have proved ephemeral and would now be ridiculed by the critics. Their stale plots with familiar situations were then taken without complaint as a matter of playhouse routine by the devotees of the drama. So long as their favourite players strolled and intoned with a formidable strength in the manner of Macready or flashed lightning with the fiery and dynamic genius of Edmund Kean they were amply satisfied. In an anonymous book of essays called *The Old Playgoer*, which represents the opinions of an assiduous as well as experienced member of the early Victorian audience in London, there is scarcely any mention of the play; the critical attention is centred wholly on performance. So the book is really misnamed. It should be *The Old Player-goer*. It was the voice, the gesture, the mien, and the energy of the actor that filled the theatre and kept the drama solvent and, at the best, prosperous. The words that were spoken and the tale that was told did not matter. What was wanted was a personal richness and bravura both in the comic parts and in the tragic ones, into whose performance the player went as it were with drums beating and flags flying. The word 'ham', fashionable in our time for the denigration of uninhibited acting, was not known. If it had been, the audience would have cried out for a diet of 'ham' without stint.

There was an abundance of stage-struck youth, callow lads for the most part, who not only wanted to see Macbeth or King Richard III on the stage but to shout and bellow in these roles themselves. Boz gives a contemptuous picture of their antics in the thirteenth of his *Sketches*, called *Private Theatres*. In these, managers of a seedy kind sold opportunities to the ambitious and unskilled tyro, who would put up a pound or two for the chance to play a large part or a few shillings for a small one.

> 'RICHARD THE THIRD.—DUKE OF GLO'STER, 2*l.*; EARL OF RICHMOND, 1*l.*; DUKE OF BUCKINGHAM, 15*s.*; CATESBY, 12*s.*; TRESSEL, 10*s.* 6*d.*; LORD STANLEY, 5*s.*; LORD MAYOR OF LONDON, 2*s.* 6*d.*'
>
> Such [wrote Boz] are the written placards wafered up in the gentlemen's dressing-room, or the green-room (where there is any), at a private theatre; and such are the sums extracted from the shop-till, or overcharged in the office expenditure, by the donkeys who are prevailed upon to pay for permission to exhibit their lamentable ignorance and boobyism on the stage of a private theatre. This they do, in proportion to the scope afforded by the character for the display of their imbecility. For instance, the Duke of Glo'ster is well worth two pounds, because he has it all to himself; he must wear a real sword, and what is better still, he must draw it, several times in the course of the piece. The soliloquies alone are well worth fifteen shillings; then there is the stabbing King Henry—decidedly cheap at three-and-sixpence, that's eighteen-and-sixpence; bullying the coffin-bearers—say eighteenpence, though it's worth much more—that's a pound. Then the love scene with Lady Ann, and the bustle of the fourth act, can't be dear at ten shillings more—that's only one pound ten, including the 'off with his head!'—which is sure to bring down the applause, and it is very easy to do—'Orf with his ed' (very quick and loud;—then slow and sneeringly)—'So much for Bu-u-uckingham!'

Incidentally the 'Off with his head' line is not in Shakespeare at all. It was an eighteenth-century insertion and very popular.

The fees paid by the aspiring mummers were the management's reward, since naturally few, except some friends of the performers, would pay to see such a massacre of a great play. Plenty of drama was included, farce as well as tragedy. The performance went on for six hours or so. The more that was acted, the more was the money paid by the eager and exhibitionist youngsters.

With no competition from the powerful alternative of the films, or from the radio and television, which have followed the film as rivals to the actor appearing in person, there was a ready public for drama of all kinds. After a distinguished start as the Royal Cobourg Theatre, with spectacular plays and some Shakespeare, that house, under the name of the Victoria, became a favourite resort of a huge and rowdy audience fed with farces, melodramas, songs, and dancing. Mayhew gave several pages in his book about London life to 'The Vic Gallery' as it was round about 1850. Entrance to 'the gods' cost threepence and the long staircase leading up to their tumultuous heaven was crowded with a queue of 'costers' before the opening. It was a young audience, according to this account, chiefly composed of lads and girls and young mothers with their babies (the infants, poor wretches, got in for a penny halfpenny), and it was a hungry one too. The 'ham-sandwich men and pig-trotter women' did a brisk trade all night and there was much throwing of orange-peel and nutshells.

Mayhew said that the Vic gallery held as many as fifteen hundred or two thousand people, but this is almost incredible as a London theatre of average size now seats about a thousand in all. If there were as many as fifteen hundred in this amphitheatre the crowding must have been intense and the heated atmosphere repulsive. It is recounted that most of the men took off their coats, showing their braces or 'bare shoulders peeping out of ragged shirts'. In the accommodation of great numbers there were 'piles of boys on each others' shoulders at the back'. It was a theatre-loving age, in the back streets of south London as well as with 'the quality' to the north of the river.

Both the entertainment and the reception of it varied widely. 'Vigorous exercise was preferred to any emotional speech. The child of the storm's declaration that she would share her father's death or imprisonment as a matter of duty had no effect at all compared with the split in the horn-pipe and, when a powerful heroine threw down four Russian soldiers in a melodrama, cries of "Go to it, my tulip" resounded from every throat.'

Dances and comic songs in which the audience could join were particularly popular and there were therefore plenty of these amid the acted pieces. Later the Vic, having become notorious for drunkenness as well as din, was rescued by Miss Emma Cons, who was succeeded by her niece, Lilian Baylis. Under their ruling the house became the Royal Victoria Hall and Coffee Tavern, teetotal and uplifting with its lectures and good music. Next it was the Old Vic Theatre, at first devoted to opera at popular prices, later to Shakespeare, and now the nucleus of the National Theatre.

In the serious theatre of the time William Charles Macready (1793–1873) was not only a sovereign figure but a close friend and correspondent of Dickens. His ungovernable temper was his enemy and led to the making of enemies in plenty, especially among actors of whom he was rudely critical. But his sense of what was due to the proper presentation of the English drama was a lofty one and he did not offer Shakespeare merely as a raree-show for the eye or a vehicle for personal display. While Macready was supreme at the centre of things Edmund Phelps was doing work of sterling worth for Shakespeare at Sadler's Wells on the slopes that led up to Islington, where he saved the texts as Shakespeare wrote them from the absurd distortions to which they had been submitted by players who thought they knew better than the poet.

The Wells had begun its long life as a pleasure-garden beside a medicinal spring in 1683. When Sadler retired in 1699 he left a 'Musick House' as well as a popular resort and these were taken over by one Miles, who let it become a scene of very odd and sometimes disgusting entertainments. The public could here watch a man who for a wager of five pounds would eat a live cock, feathers, entrails, and all, sauced in oil and vinegar, and washed down with half a pint of brandy. A Mr Rosoman, a local builder, took the place over in 1746 and later substituted a large theatre for the Musick Room. He encouraged the public by offering a box for three shillings with port or punch laid on in some quantity and for nothing. Pit and gallery cost one shilling and sixpence and a shilling, and in both cases another sixpence purchased a pint of either drink.

Dickens's connection with Sadler's Wells began with his editing of the Memoirs of Grimaldi, the celebrated clown who had been the darling of the Wells and the star performer in its pantomimes. He added a preface and supervised the book for Bentley, whose magazine, *Bentley's Miscellany*, he was then editing, himself contributing *Oliver Twist* in monthly parts. Dickens cannot have seen Grimaldi at his best since the great clown made his farewell performance in 1828. Grimaldi belonged to the age, and enjoyed the praise, of Charles Lamb. His Christian name was Joseph and his triumphs gave the name Joey to clowns for years to come.

To the temperament of Dickens all eccentric and exceptional people and things were naturally congenial. In clowning of the first class he delighted and he gave an enthusiastic description of Astley's Amphitheatre, which housed a famous circus and assorted dramatic spectacles. In the eleventh of the Boz *Sketches* he described his own boyish joy and a family's delight beside the ring where the great Ducrow was later to be the star horseman of the day. We meet the splendid ring-master, 'who always wears a military uniform with a table-cloth inside the breast of his coat, in which costume he forcibly reminds one of a fowl trussed for roasting'. He has badinage with the clown, who treats him to back-answers and ludicrous grimaces while cutting fantastic capers.

Astley's was three times burned down and always rapidly re-

'Mazeppa'

built, so keen was the demand for its displays of all kind. One of its panoramic and equestrian spectacles which Dickens and other writers including Swinburne especially enjoyed was called 'Mazeppa'. The star was Adah Menken, an American dancer and showgirl who became an actress with rare skill in horsemanship. In this audacious display she shocked some of the public and won the admiration and even adoration of the rest by galloping tied to the back of a wild horse, and that 'in a state of virtual nudity'. The lady's life was as adventurous in affairs of the heart as it was in the perils and triumphs of her work in the saddle. Her London success as Mazeppa was in 1864 and she was the talk of the town during the last years of Dickens's life. Astley's had thrilled him as a boy and did so once more in his maturity. Later it was taken over by the circus proprietor known as 'Lord' George Sanger and survived till 1895, more than a century after Philip Astley had established it beside Westminster Bridge. It had drawn a faithful audience to its ring or its stage and was one of the essential sights for families on a London visit as well as for Londoners themselves.

Circus folk come into the grim industrial scenery of *Hard Times*, and the contrast between the kind-heartedness of their wandering, impoverished, and courageous lives and the dreary mixture of avarice and respectability in the ruling class of Coketown was naturally stressed by an author who so much preferred a clown in the sawdust to the kind of capitalist whom Gradgrind's economic theories were promoting to power.

There was poor Jupe, a clown who was failing or, in circus lingo, 'missed his tip at the banners and was loose in his ponging and so was goosed', which had to be interpreted to Gradgrind and Bounderby as 'short in his leaps and bad in his tumbling' and therefore hissed by the audience. There was E. W. B. Childers,

> so justly celebrated for his daring vaulting act as the Wild Huntsman of the North American Prairies; in which popular performance, a diminutive boy with an old face, who now accompanied him, assisted as his infant son: being carried upside down over his father's shoulder, by one foot, and held by the crown of his head, heels upwards, in the palm of his father's hand, according to the violent paternal manner in which wild huntsmen may be observed to fondle their offspring.

In the company assembled by the boss and ring-master, Mr Sleary,

> There were two or three handsome young women among them, with their two or three husbands, and their two or three mothers, and their

eight or nine little children, who did the fairy business when required. The father of one of the families was in the habit of balancing the father of another of the families on the top of a great pole; the father of a third family often made a pyramid of both those fathers, with Master Kidderminster for the apex, and himself for the base; all the fathers could dance upon rolling casks, stand upon bottles, catch knives and balls, twirl hand-basins, ride upon anything, jump over everything, and stick at nothing. All the mothers could (and did) dance, upon the slack wire and the tight-rope, and perform rapid acts on bare-backed steeds; none of them were at all particular in respect of showing their legs; and one of them, alone in a Greek chariot, drove six in hand into every town they came to. They were not very tidy in their private dresses, they were not at all orderly in their domestic arrangements, and the combined literature of the whole company would have produced but a poor letter on any subject. Yet there was a remarkable gentleness and childishness about these people, a special inaptitude for any kind of sharp practice, and an untiring readiness to help and pity one another, deserving often of as much respect, and always of as much generous construction, as the every-day virtues of any class of people in the world.'

Dickens was a man of quick and emotional reactions. He was as ready to 'goose' Gradgrind and give Bounderby a kick behind as he was to applaud the general behaviour of the Sleary troupe and pat the nervous and inadequate Jupe upon the back.

There is not much play-going in the novels but in *Nicholas Nickleby* there is plenty of play-acting. The touring manager, Mr Vincent Crummles, Mrs Crummles, and their daughter, the Infant Phenomenon, who is cut down to size despite girlhood's advancing years by abundant doses of gin and water, which may or may not have provided the required check on growth, are grandly absurd, and their portraits may be three parts accurate as a description of mummers on the road. We must allow for some heightened colour and writing for the laugh. But glorious writing it is, and the Crummles family, along with Miss Snevellicci, 'who could do anything, from a medley dance to Lady Macbeth, and also always played some part in blue silk knee-smalls at her benefit', Miss Belvawney, 'who seldom aspired to speaking parts', and 'the unrivalled Miss Petowker of the Theatre Royal Drury Lane', famous as 'The Blood Drinker' and 'the only sylph who could stand upon one leg and play the tambourine on her other knee *like* a sylph', provide some of the richest comedy that Dickens ever wrote.

Nor are the jealous and petulant men of the company less amusing. There is probably something close to the common practice of the time in the Crummles method of finding plays. When Nicholas joins at Portsmouth the Crummles 'corps', as Mrs Crummles calls it, he is regarded as an educated fellow who should be able to manage a bit of writing and have a piece ready by Monday morning.

'Upon my word,' said Nicholas, taking the manager aside, 'I don't think I can be ready by Monday.'

'Pooh, pooh,' replied Mr Crummles.

'But really I can't,' returned Nicholas; 'my invention is not accustomed to these demands, or possibly I might produce——'

'Invention! what the devil's that got to do with it?' cried the manager, hastily.

'Everything, my dear sir.'

'Nothing, my dear sir,' retorted the manager, with evident impatience. 'Do you understand French?'

'Perfectly well.'

'Very good,' said the manager, opening the table-drawer, and giving a roll of paper from it to Nicholas. 'There! Just turn that into English, and put your name on the title-page.'

Stealing plays was a common habit. The English theatre then

lifted much of its material from France and there were no strict laws of copyright to prevent such theft. It was a robbery which applied to books as well as plays and Dickens himself suffered a great deal from American pillage of his books, which were widely printed and read without a penny of payment. The same experience was met in the eighteen-seventies by Gilbert and Sullivan, whose early operettas were pirated without shame.

Nicholas was further requested by the male members of the 'corps' to provide suitable parts for their talents, and of course a role for the Infant. He had also to include a scene introducing such properties as Mr Crummles carries with him, a pump and tub. He was then casually told to study the parts of Romeo, Rover, Cassio, and Jeremy Diddler with the intimation that he could easily 'knock them off' since 'one part helps the other so much'. Romeo was astonishingly mastered in a few days and successfully performed by Nicholas, who had no theatrical experience at all. It would be a cut and mangled version of Shakespeare's tragedy, mangled both in text and performance, but it was received by the Portsmouth public with 'hearty plaudits and unbounded fervour and Smike was pronounced unanimously, alike by audience and actors, the very prince and prodigy of Apothecaries'. Since Shakespeare's Mantuan apothecary 'had famine in his cheeks' and 'sharp misery had worn him to the bone' the wretched victim of Mr Squeers's diet and discipline must certainly have looked the part.

The remuneration of a touring player was then very small. Nicholas was offered and accepted a pound a week for his joint services as actor and author; it is not made certain whether such aid as Smike could render was thrown in for good measure with no added shilling or so. If we can judge by the rates of pay in the touring companies and a little earlier that was not bad remuneration for a novice. Mr and Mrs Butler's company, which included Richmond in Swaledale in its Yorkshire circuit at the end of the

The great bespeak for Miss Snevellicci. 'The people in the Borum box rose as one man'—*Nicholas Nickleby*

eighteenth century, paid fifteen shillings a week to players of experience and out of this board and victuals had to be found. The travels from town to town were arduous, especially in the north, where the journeys were long and often mountainous. The 'principals' might drive with the costumes and such scenery and 'props' as were carried. But there was much foot-slogging for the others.

The companies were usually formed with a family nucleus.

The Crummles family would be a broad caricature of the Butlers and the Wallises in Yorkshire. Nicholas and Smike met the great Vincent with his sons twelve miles outside Portsmouth, and the whole party was packed along with the dresses and 'props' in 'a vehicle of unknown design', spoken of as a phaeton. This was hauled by a long-suffering pony whose mother, said Mr Crummles acting as coachman, had also had stage experience. 'She ate apple-pie at a circus for upwards of fourteen years . . . fired pistols, and went to bed in a nightcap; and, in short, took the low comedy entirely.' Mrs Crummles and the Infant Phenomenon met them at Portsmouth.

Precocious children were great favourites in the theatre of the period. There was a phenomenon in the Butler's company, as there was in others. She was Jane Fielding Wallis, whose father said of her when she was thirteen, 'She is supposed to be the greatest theatrical genius in the world. She is a Prodigy.' (We are not far away from Mr Crummles and his claims for his girl genius.) Nowadays the boy marvel is usually a singer or crooner of the disc world and fantastically rewarded for what may be a small-enough talent. But the phenomenon of those days had long parts to learn and was obliged to prove his or her capacity in classic drama.

The most remarkable of the prodigies was a boy called West, who took the stage under the name of Master Betty. In 1804 at the age of thirteen he played the great Shakespearian roles at Drury Lane and Covent Garden. Such was his success and his renown that at the instance of the Prime Minister the House of Commons adjourned to see him as Hamlet. But he was the comet of a very short season and the victim of a capricious and even brutal public. Judging him to have failed as Richard III, hardly an easy part for a boy, the audience 'goosed' him. Hissed off the stage, he never managed to re-establish himself and retired to a long life of poverty and obscurity; born in 1791, he died four years after Dickens, in 1874.

Ninetta Crummles, the Infant Phenomenon introduced to Nicholas and described by her father as possessing a talent not to be imagined, and receiving letters of praise from the nobility and gentry of almost every town in England, was more a dancer and a pirouettist than an actress. But she is representative of the curious world of the early nineteenth-century theatre, in which such a career as that of Master Betty was possible. With our boys wailing into microphones to the hysterical ecstasy of their 'fans' we are in no position to laugh at the prodigy craze, which Dickens satirised in his picture of Ninetta Crummles.

The pitifully small wage of the players was relieved with occasional benefit performances, which were not limited only to the manager and his family. The entire takings at one of these benefits or 'bespeaks' went to the one recipient. Such arrangements were necessary to keep the members of the touring company together and to save them from the extremes of poverty. Before the performance there was much canvassing of the likely play-goers in the town in order to coax them into 'bespeaking' seats. For Miss Snevellicci's great night Nicholas was persuaded to join the campaign of salesmanship in household visiting, and he helped to dispose of three box seats at half a crown apiece after asking three shillings for them.

The prices in the theatres outside London were usually three shillings for a place in a box, two shillings for a place in the pit, and a shilling for a climb to the gallery. But these might be raised for the 'bespeak' of a favourite artist. When we remember the cost of living at that period and the ability of an actor to find bed and board and keep clothed for fifteen shillings a week, these prices seem quite high. Assuming that money then bought ten times as much as it does today, a moderate estimate, then the price of box seats was the equivalent of thirty shillings while the gallery seats could be sold for the equivalent of ten. Comparing the price-lists of various epochs always leads to some puzzling results because people set such different values on different kinds of articles at different times. For example, Henslowe, an Elizabethan theatre manager at the time of Shakespeare, would pay as much for one gorgeous robe for a royal part as he would for the sole rights in three or four five-act plays. But however we look at it, the early Victorian public were ready to pay substantially for their night at a theatre. They demanded a very long night for their money, including a tragedy, a farce, and incidental music and dancing.

The takings in the country towns were severely limited by the smallness of the theatres. The illustration by Phiz of 'the great bespeak for Miss Snevellicci' shows a tiny auditorium and this is supported by the example of the Richmond (Yorkshire) Theatre already mentioned. This has survived the chances and changes of dramatic history and of local ups and downs since 1788. It has recently been saved from neglect and most handsomely renovated in its original form for present use. In the drawing by Phiz of the Portsmouth Theatre the stage juts well forward towards a pit of perhaps eight rows: round and slightly above this are the lower boxes, one section of which is packed with as many people as a thrifty family could cram into the space they had bespoken. Over this is the gallery. The attendance is sadly small, but Phiz was evidently depicting the start of the affair since Dickens wrote that the audience 'increased considerably' during the evening. But the latecomers would not be so profitable to Miss Snevellicci because there was a general rule of half-prices at half-time.

The Richmond Theatre closely resembles the type and size of play-house shown in the illustration. It is very small and when one reads of an audience of three hundred one is astonished that so many could have been contained. One explanation is that people were generally smaller a century or two centuries ago than they are now and needed less leg room. Also they appeared to take crowding and discomfort with equanimity, sitting, if the play was a success, jammed on narrow, hard, backless benches in the pit and gallery and with very little space in the boxes. The tradition of gladly enduring discomfort in the theatre, especially in the cheaper parts, is not yet dead, but the superior amenity offered by the cinema to payers of even the lowest price has at last had some effect and procured alterations. When Dickens went to the play as a youngster he must have been used to jostling and cramping and expected nothing better. It was not, except in wealthy homes, an age of cushioned ease. The coach journeys and the earliest kind of travel by train accustomed passengers to sitting cold and sitting hard; but wedged on their play-house benches they would not be shivering.

The history of a great theatrical family recounted by Miss Marguerite Steen in her book *A Pride of Terrys* begins in the town where Nicholas made his stage appearance with Mr Crummles. There Benjamin Terry, gay, feckless, a ready comedian but never a star performer himself, took in 1838 an admirable wife in Sarah Ballard, whose children, like her endurances, were many. The couple toured in the hard way and in the midst of their travels and toils they bred a large family. Of Mrs Terry's eleven children two died in infancy and four rose to high, even the highest, positions on the stage. The earliest were born in the course of their professional wanderings, Kate at Falmouth, Ellen at Coventry. Kate rose rapidly to be a leading actress in London. Dickens saw her in 1863, when she was nineteen, appearing in what he called 'a small part in a picturesque French drama' and he wrote to Macready, 'she has a tender love-scene in this piece which is a really beautiful and artistic thing. . . . I told Fechter "that is the very best piece of womanly tenderness I have ever seen on the stage and you'll find that no audience can miss it".' (Fechter was a French actor who had great success in London in the eighteen-sixties.) Kate soon left the stage for a prosperous marriage. As Mrs Lewis she was the mother of Mrs Frank Gielgud, who was the mother of Sir John Gielgud. So this great actor is a direct descendant of the early Victorian theatre in which the Terrys rose and shone.

Mrs Benjamin Terry's second daughter and Sir John's great-aunt was Ellen, of rare beauty, accomplishment, and renown. Born in 1847, she appeared as a child actress at the age of nine. A promising career was interrupted by an early and unhappy marriage to the painter G. F. Watts and by subsequent motherhood. Thus Dickens could not see her in the fullness of her fascination. It was later, with Henry Irving, that she was to be the leading actress of the day and the wonder of the town. Miss Steen's account of the lives and careers of the Terry parents and their children gives a vivid picture of the early Victorian theatre which Dickens knew in his youth, and it to some extent contradicts the picture of the Crummles 'corps' and its way of life. For some reason Miss Steen objects to Dickens as a foppish young man in lacquered boots and fancy waistcoats; but there is no harm in taking pride in appearance and a genius can surely be excused a taste for looking his best, even if he overdoes the observance of elegance. The behaviour of Crummles may be a libel on the profession which the Terrys were to

Kate Terry

adorn, but as a piece of fiction he and the troupe are unforgettable.

With the Terrys we also meet the theatre as Dickens was to know it later in London. It was a theatre which had some well-contrived play-writing, particularly by his friend Edward Bulwer-Lytton, author of *The Lady of Lyons* and *Money*, work not esteemed or revived now but long surviving as popular successes in the Victorian era.

A new note was introduced by Tom Robertson in the eighteen-sixties. He chose one-word titles, such as *Society*, *Ours*, *Caste*, *Play*, and *School*, and avoided the more flowery and rhetorical style of dialogue as well as the familiar tricks of melodrama. He introduced domestic scenes produced with realistic settings and together with his chief interpreters, Squire Bancroft and his very talented wife Marie Wilton, met with great success. There was a public ready for this comparatively quiet form of entertainment and ready to pay well to see it. Bancroft could charge ten shillings and sixpence for a stall and had made enough to retire on in his early forties. Crummles would have thought rather poorly of Robertson's method of writing and very highly of the money he could draw into the theatre. The Bancrofts were friends of Dickens and one of the last letters that he wrote, on 31 May 1870, was to thank Marie Wilton for some medicine which she had recommended. He ended, 'Whether this remedy succeeds or fails as to the neuralgia, I shall always consider myself under an obligation to it for having indirectly procured me the great pleasure of receiving a communication from you; for I hope I may lay claim to being one of the most earnest and delighted of your many artistic admirers.' Miss Wilton was regarded as a brilliant and charming comedienne. Her talent and the plays in which she appeared were drawing a wider audience of the middle class, whose members did not need the old sensationalism or 'ham' acting to attract them to a theatre. The change in dramatic method from the grandiose to the natural style had not passed Dickens by or left him unaffected.

Amateur acting has already been described at its lowest level in the deplorable exhibitions of the lads who bought their roles in the private theatres. There was not then the extremely wide range of performance, some of it excellent in quality as well as ambitious in its choice of play, which is now to be found all over the country. But there was in the kind of society which Dickens frequented after his early success in life a great eagerness to write and act in plays for the pleasure and excitement of the exercise. Since Dickens can fairly be considered as a diverted, if not frustrated, professional actor he was eager to write, to perform, and to produce theatricals in his own home.

It is one of the marvels of Dickens's immense vitality that amid all his writing of books, articles, short stories, and innumerable letters he could find time and energy not only for memorising and acting big parts but for the tiresome business of organising the amateur performances which he so much enjoyed. In 1845, while he was working at the foundation of a London daily newspaper, the *Daily News*, he gathered his friends to appear in Ben Jonson's comedy *Every Man in His Humour*. Forster, his close friend and biographer, Cruikshank, his illustrator, Douglas Jerrold, Mark Lemon and Leech of *Punch*, together with two of Dickens's brothers, were recruited for the cast and rehearsed by Macready. A performance was given at the Royalty Theatre and repeated before the Prince Consort and an audience truly to be described as 'nobility and gentry'. Of course some of the wits were sarcastic. At the first performance Lord Melbourne damned the dullness of the affair and that audibly during the interval.

Jane Welsh Carlyle, who could be waspish, was there in Macready's box and wrote about it to her husband. She thought that Jerrold did best and that Dickens as Captain Bobadil and Forster as

Kitely were on a par. 'Poor little Dickens', she wrote, mocking his effort to affect the voice of a man of six feet. (But do six-footers always have tremendous voices?) She added that she found 'a tall man leant to a wall, with his head touching the ceiling like a caryatid, to all appearance asleep or resolutely trying it under the most unfavourable circumstances'. This was Tennyson. It was certainly what the papers could fairly call 'a distinguished gathering'. And we need not be too much impressed by the sneers of the supercilious. The probability is that 'poor little Dickens' gave a capable display.

In 1856, while in the midst of another substantial masterpiece, *Little Dorrit*, Dickens made a miniature theatre out of the schoolroom of Tavistock House in Bloomsbury, where he had been living since 1852. There he produced in the following January *The Frozen Deep*, a drama of artistic exploration written by Wilkie Collins with the help of Dickens, who played a principal part and also composed the prologue. Sir John Franklin, seeking the North-West Passage through the north Atlantic to the Pacific, had died in the attempt. The icy and tragic subject was topical. The scenery and lighting effects were elaborate. Clarkson Stanfield, the chief scene-painter of the day, arrived with seventy pots of paint. Several members of the family had parts. There was lavish entertainment for all and lavish melodramatics for the audience. Dickens, as a noble explorer, died under a Union Jack and reduced to tears an audience more ready to be thus powerfully affected by strong emotional histrionics than we are today. There was only room for fifty spectators, but these included Queen Victoria, Prince Albert, and the King of the Belgians. With a strengthened cast and professional actresses replacing the Dickens girls *The Frozen Deep* was played publicly at the Free Trade Hall in Manchester in the following August.

There was evidently no feeling that amateurs were rushing too boldly into the professional field, and as reader and actor of his own works Dickens became what he had secretly longed to be, as professional as any soloist and one who could be a whole company in his own person. He had absorbed as a constant spectator the essence of projecting all types of character and all modes of feeling. From his boyhood relish of the circus and the Crummles vein, from his later and close friendship with Macready, and from his playgoing in the central London theatres he had constantly learned the tricks of the trade while he enjoyed watching them and their potency. He did not ask, because none asked then, that the theatre should be the forum for plays of ideas and a vehicle for propagating his Radical and reformist opinions. The theatre of Ibsen and Shaw he might in the end perhaps have come to like, since it could be used to expose the kind of humbug and injustice which he had pilloried in his novels. But the New Drama of this penetrative and campaigning kind came some time after his death. The theatre of his day was flamboyant, but the flames that it kindled were in the heart and did not enlighten the brain. It may seem odd to us that while he was glorying in the sentimental heroics of *The Frozen Deep* he was simultaneously arraigning bourgeois society, the reckless greed of the new capitalism, and the incompetence and corruption of the English ruling class. But to nobody in Dickens's time was it conceivable that the theatre should be an arsenal for the munitions of a social upheaval.

CHAPTER SIX

Getting About

READERS who relate the novels of Dickens to the dates at which they appeared are naturally surprised to find that his characters are still travelling by horse-driven coach years after railway trains had begun to roar across the country. (The trains, when they do penetrate the story as in *Dombey and Son*, are roaring monsters to the author.) The reason for this back-dating, which made Dickens write in 1860 about the England of 1830, is probably an obsession with his own childhood which he was unable to throw off. To an acutely sensitive and impressionable boy the early years had been bewildering in the sudden change from comparative security and contentment to poverty and despair.

There was that happy enough childhood in Rochester where, between the ages of five and twelve, he had a teacher aware of his pupil's talents, books to read, the bustle of the streets with their coaches and taverns to gaze at, and the rich Kent country characters to overhear. There was Chatham and its nautical life near by; there was the ambience of ancient Rochester itself with castle and cathedral looming above him. There was the Medway valley and there were the Kentish hop-fields and orchards close and invitingly beside him. Just as small boys were to become ardent and industrious 'train-spotters' later on and to remain so when motor cars were travelling much faster than trains, so one can see the boy Charles as a coach-spotter fascinated by the clatter of the traffic as it came and went on the London road, with the horses steaming and the driver in full conversation when a stop was made and refreshments taken.

So it happened that Dickens never wholly grew out of that boyhood, and when he looked for the circumstance and scenery of a story his mind turned instinctively to the Kent and the Camden Town and the lawyer's offices which he had known even before he was sixteen. In his last book, *The Mystery of Edwin Drood*, on which he was working when he died in 1870, we are back not only in Rochester but in the Rochester of the stage-coach. Cloisterham he called it then and this Cloisterham is a dark scene of sinister events; the atmosphere is macabre with its hoarse cathedral bell and its rooks hovering and cawing round the tower. Yet it drew him back, back in time as well as in locality, to the days when 'there was a coach melodiously called Timpson's Blue-Eyed Maid instead of a locomotive engine severely called No. 97—belonging to the South Eastern Railway, and spitting ashes and hot water over the blighted ground'. When he had important visitors at Gad's Hill he would arrange for one of the now vanished stage-coaches 'with a couple of postillions in the old red jacket of the Dover Road' to be fetched out and so carry them round the sights. Thus he entertained the American poet Longfellow, who incidentally shared with him a tributary admiration for the village blacksmith. Joe Gargery in *Great Expectations* would have been a congenial character to this guest at Gad's Hill.

The great days of coaching were nearly over when Dickens was beginning to write. The railways overtook him and for a while he obviously did not welcome them. A year after his birth in 1812 steam-power had been used for traction on lines beside a colliery and in the following year the first locomotive constructed by George Stephenson travelled at the rate of six miles an hour. In September 1825 the Stockton and Darlington railway was opened. In 1830 came the Liverpool and Manchester line. The north was ahead of the south and it was not until 1838 that trains were running from London to Birmingham. The London to

Brighton service began in 1841 and then came a decade of general expansion. There was huge prosperity for some of the promoters and wild gambling in the shares of railway companies with gains and losses mixed. Consequently when after the essays and tales of Boz the first chapters of *The Pickwick Papers* were appearing in 1836, Dickens, as a Londoner, could hardly introduce railway travel. But he knew about it (the London to Greenwich line was just about to open) and in the heading of chapter 8 he announced that what followed would be 'strongly illustrative of the position that love is not a railway-train'. In *Master Humphrey's Clock* (1840) Mr Weller, the coach-driver, denounces the new railway engine as 'a nasty wheezin', gaspin', puffin', bustin' monster, always out o' breath, with a shiny green-and-gold back like an unpleasant beetle'. When six years later Dickens got to work on *Dombey and Son* the monster is hard at work too, roaring in and out of Euston on the line that had been constructed right under Dickens's old school, Wellington House in the Hampstead Road, and carrying Mr Dombey and Major Bagstock on their trip to Leamington.

So until 1841 the Londoner travelling to Brighton had to go by coach and not until 1844 could he take train to Dover. The London to Brighton coaches were frequent and fast, and a business man who did not mind spending ten hours in a coach (in two spells of five hours) could leave his Brighton home or hotel in the early morning, see to his affairs in the City, and be back the same night. But with speed came danger. The coaches could topple over. In the piece by Boz called *The Tuggses at Ramsgate* the family are discussing a seaside holiday. Margate was dismissed as full of trades-people. When Brighton was mentioned, 'Mr Cymon Tuggs opposed an insurmountable objection. All the coaches had been upset, in turn, within the last three weeks; each had averaged two passengers killed and six wounded: and, in every case, the newspapers had distinctly understood that no blame whatever was

'All the coaches had been upset in the last three weeks'—Boz, *The Tuggses*

attributed to the coachman.' Boz was a humorist and we need not take his casualty figures seriously. But there would have been no point in these remarks if there had not been frequent and serious accidents. The Tuggses decide to go to Ramsgate: it could be safely as well as conveniently reached by steamer.

Travel by steamship had preceded the railway journey by a considerable period of time. The first idea of steam navigation had been set forth in a patent obtained by Jonathan Hulls in 1736, but nothing came of that. There was an experiment with steam navigation on the Thames in 1801 but no regular sailings were made. Scotland was just ahead of England in providing a passenger service by steamboat. In 1812 Henry Bell's *Comet* went from Glasgow to Greenock and back three times a week at a speed of seven and a half miles an hour. There were steamboats on the Thames in 1814.

In 1821 *The Rising Star*, a steamer built by Lord Cochrane, crossed the Atlantic. Progress after that was rapid and general. In April 1838 *The Great Western* steamed from Bristol to New York in sixteen days.

Thus in the early eighteen-thirties to go to Ramsgate by water was the normal way of starting a holiday. The Tuggses sat in comfort with a band playing and lunched on cold pigeon-pie and sherry. Dickens, though retaining his fondness for the horse on the road, had no sentimental attachment to the sailing-ships that were rapidly being replaced by what Charles Lamb called contemptuously 'the foppery and fresh-water niceness of the modern steam-packet'. In his essay on *The Old Margate Hoy* (a hoy was a sailing-ship used for carrying passengers on short journeys) Lamb, in a very flowery and affected style, addressed that vessel with 'its rough accommodations' thus: 'To the winds and waves thou committedst thy goodly freightage and didst ask no aid of magic fumes and spells and boiling cauldrons. With the gales of heaven thou wentest swimmingly: or, when it was their pleasure, stoodest still with sailor-like patience. Thy course was natural, not forced, as in a hot-bed; nor didst thou go poisoning the breath of ocean with sulphurous smoke.' That was written in 1823. Dickens grew up with steam on the water but not with steam on land and he took the former for granted. Assuming that his Tuggses went to Ramsgate a dozen years after Lamb's enraptured description of the Margate hoy, the family had forgotten, if it ever appreciated, the joys of the 'rough accommodations' and of the kind of navigation which had to stop in a storm and let the passengers ride it out with what 'sailor-like patience' they possessed, which was probably none at all. They enjoyed the tinkle of the band, the sherry and the pigeon-pie, and the 'foppery' despised by Lamb when assuming the role of a tough old salt.

Dickens experienced a larger and much less pleasant kind of

travel when he went to America in 1842. Rashly he chose to go in the month of January, when the north Atlantic can provide its roughest and most agonising of crossings. Those who travel in one of the largest and best equipped of modern liners can be made distressingly aware of that. Charles and his wife Kate took passages on the *Britannia*, a three-master with one very tall funnel and huge paddles. It was a vessel of only 1,154 tons and would be thought small for a Channel passage today. The weather was abominable and their sufferings severe.

In chapter 15 of *Martin Chuzzlewit* the memories of that journey, which took sixteen days from Liverpool to Halifax, Nova Scotia, are written in prose that heaves and groans with the tossed and straining timbers of the tiny but indomitable ship. The *Screw*, as it is called in the narrative, carried many emigrants in the steerage as well as its cabin passengers, since the rush for the New World of supposed opportunity was on and many who could scrape up the fare were packed into the narrow space, bringing their own provisions and cooking and eating as they could, if they had any appetite for doing so.

The *Britannia* going to America. 'In a month we shall be there'
Martin Chuzzlewit

A dark, low, stifling cabin, surrounded by berths all filled to overflowing with men, women, and children, in various stages of sickness and misery, is not the liveliest place of assembly at any time; but when it is so crowded (as the steerage cabin of the *Screw* was every passage out), that mattresses and beds are heaped upon the floor, to the extinction of everything like comfort, cleanliness, and decency, it is liable to operate, and not only as a pretty strong barrier against amiability of temper, but as a positive encourager of selfish and rough humours. . . .

There were English people, Irish people, Welsh people, and Scotch people there, all with their little store of coarse food and shabby clothes, and nearly all with their families of children. There were children of all ages, from the baby at the breast, to the slattern girl who was as much a grown woman as her mother. Every kind of domestic suffering that is bred in poverty, illness, banishment, sorrow, and long travel in bad weather, was crammed into the little space; and yet was there infinitely less of complaint and querulousness, and infinitely more of mutual assistance and general kindness to be found in that unwholesome ark, than in many brilliant ball-rooms.

Although Dickens was a cabin passenger he was extremely glad to leave the ship at Boston, whither it had come from Halifax with the seas still stormy. He had no reason to feel the sentiments of a maritime race about the exhilaration of an ocean trip. His view on landing was probably that which he put in the mouth of Mark Tapley: 'And this is the land of Liberty, is it? Very well. I'm agreeable. Any land will do for me after so much water.'

But he was to sail again when he was fifty-five and in failing health. That was in November 1867, but the passage of his ship, the *Cuba*, was quicker. Halifax was cut out and Boston reached in ten days; he returned to England in the following April with better weather; his friends said that he arrived looking tanned with the fresh air and seeming years younger. This was a far too hopeful view, for the exertions of his recital tour had sapped and not stimulated his once demonic energy. Back in Kent, however, he busied himself with hospitality, including the reception of Longfellow and the coach-drives already mentioned. The trains were becoming general, but for entertainment let the world of Mr Weller return amid a sounding of the horn and clatter of hooves.

Because the horses go clip-clopping on the roads to and from London even in the later stories there is no reason to suppose that Dickens took only a Christmas-card and sentimental view of his boyhood's mode of travel. If there were women to occupy the interior of the coach and the men had only the outside seats for occupation in wintry weather, hardship was intense, and there are many journeys in the novels to record the inevitable feats of endurance. When Nicholas Nickleby drove north with Mr Squeers and the wretched boys who were being taken to Dotheboys Hall, they drove all day through the snow and got as far as Grantham, where two of the outside passengers, resolving to wait for another coach on the morrow, prudently got off and took rooms at the George Hotel. 'The remainder wrapped themselves more closely in their coats and cloaks, and leaving the light and warmth of the town behind them, pillowed themselves against the luggage, and prepared, with many half-suppressed moans, again to encounter the piercing blast which swept across the open country.' Some ten miles on Nicholas was nearly thrown out of his seat by a violent jerk and the coach tilted and turned over with a lady screaming inside and the horses plunging in the snow. The horses when unharnessed bolted back by themselves to the inn from which they had been taken on for the next stage, and when a careful scrutiny of the travellers was made it was ascertained that 'the lady inside had broken her lamp, and the gentleman his head; that the two front outsides had escaped with black eyes; the box with a bloody nose; the coachman with a contusion of the temple; Mr Squeers with a portmanteau bruise on his back; and the remaining passengers without any injury at all—thanks to the softness of the snow-drift in which they had been overturned'. They could walk back through the blizzard to the nearest public-house. It might be called a minor accident with light casualties. Indeed it had to be so since Dickens had to get his characters on their way to Yorkshire. But here were what are sometimes called 'the jolly old coaching days', and grim enough they could be.

The kind of disaster feared by the Tuggses as likely to be frequent on the way to Brighton could be encountered just as often on the Great North Road. In this case the snow, which had been an affliction, became something of a cushion. A slip and a crash on frozen road was a far worse risk than a tumble in the drifts. There were deaths on the road before motor cars came in and many more bumps than fatalities. The consolation of the delayed or unseated passenger was the readiness of the highway innkeeper to have blazing fires and doors ready for opening at any hour. Drinks were served steaming hot and the hams and rounds of beef were immediately on the table. There was none of the 'Too late to serve you, sir' spirit along the roads where the coaches stopped for a change of horses and for the driver and passengers to thaw their numbed limbs beside the coals and restore some inward warmth with gulps of brandy and hot water. There is an old English, or rather an English, word of Latin origin to describe this kind of refreshment. It is 'refocillate', which means literally 'to heat up the hearth with more fuel'. The members of the coaching world knew how to refocillate when journeying through a bleak frost or a wind with fangs. 'Bring in the bottled lightning' was a Dickensian request well justified by the rigours of the road in mid-winter.

As the railway began to take the traffic from the coaches in the eighteen-forties the standard of feeding declined miserably in the opinion of Dickens. The station refreshment room was a particular

A railway station refreshment room in Dickens's time

object of his hatred. In the dispersed and rather feeble story of *Mugby Junction* (1865) there is an angry contrast of the food, drink, and service available in French stations with the contemptible fare and haughty neglect of the passengers that prevailed on the English railway lines. He railed at the huge, mysterious urns which served as 'breast-works for defiant women' and the ancient sandwiches under glass domes. For another three-quarters of a century this kind of sullen supply remained prevalent on English railways and we can hardly claim that recent reforms have introduced a Continental standard of courtesy or catering. Some of the campaigns launched by Dickens were victorious; but his assault on the station urns and their dragon-like wardresses was a conspicuous failure.

He always felt that when the men of the horses gave way to the men of the machines a cordiality dwindled, and cordials, whether in a bottle or as human beings, were very much his fancy and his friends.

There is an excellent example of this roadside readiness to oblige in the description of the Saracen's Head at Towcester when Mr Pickwick with Sam Weller and friends arrived in streaming rain:

> 'There's beds here, sir,' said Sam, addressing his master, 'everything clean and comfortable. Wery good little dinner, sir, they can get ready in half an hour—pair of fowls, sir, and a weal cutlet; French beans, 'taturs, tart, and tidiness. You'd better stop vere you are, sir, if I might recommend. Take adwice, sir, as the doctor said.'

Mr Pickwick naturally decided to stop and the response was prompt and reassuring:

> 'Lights in the Sun, John; make up the fire—the gentlemen are wet!' cried the landlord. 'This way, gentlemen. Don't trouble yourself about the postboy now, sir. I'll send him to you when you ring for him, sir. Now, John, the candles.'
>
> The candles were brought, the fire was stirred up and a fresh log of wood thrown on. In ten minutes' time a waiter was laying the cloth for dinner, the curtains were drawn, the fire was blazing brightly, and everything looked (as everything always does, in all decent English inns) as if the travellers had been expected, and their comforts prepared for days beforehand.

Doubtless not all such establishments were so genially and efficiently managed, but Dickens was usually well pleased with the coaching inns and at some of their successors of today we can read his tributes to their excellence framed and displayed.

There were hardships to face. The start of a coaching day might be very early indeed. Boz gave a melancholy account of a nocturnal awakening in mid-winter and a trudge through dark and soaking streets, bag in hand, which took him to his coaching depot, the Golden Cross, at a quarter past five in the morning. The departure was to be made at six and there was hot brandy to ease the interval and to get the outside travellers, at least partially refocillated, on to the rain-swept roof of the coach. When Mr Pickwick went from London to Bath the start was fixed for half past seven in the morning from the White Horse Cellar, with hot buttered toast as well as hot drinks available. It was a drizzly day but Mr Pickwick had booked inside seats. The hundred miles to Bath were covered in under twelve hours including a brief stop for a dinner which had to be bolted. By seven in the evening the party were established in their private sitting-room in the White Hart Hotel opposite the Grand Pump Room.

To be cooped up with possibly talkative and boring company inside a coach for twelve hours could be as dismal an experience as braving the weather with an outside place. But in both cases there was the chance of achieving insensibility and a state of coma by application to the rum and brandy plentifully on hand at the early-morning start and at every stage where horses were changed.

For town travel the omnibus had arrived on the London streets in 1829, introduced by a Mr Shillibeer. The first buses were capacious and held twenty-two passengers, all inside. They were drawn by three horses trotting abreast. This kind of conveyance took up too much room in the narrow streets and had to be replaced by a smaller bus with only twelve inside and others on the roof. The bus conductor was known as a 'cad' and according to Boz (sixteenth *Sketch*) he could be a very independent and tyrannical fellow. Dickens described a bus ride along Oxford Street to the City. His cad on this occasion boasts that 'he can chuck an old gen'lm'n into the bus, shut him in, and rattle off, afore he knows vere its a-going to'.

The number of passengers was not limited to the number of seats.

> 'Any room?' cries a very hot pedestrian. 'Plenty o' room, Sir,' replies the conductor, gradually opening the door, and not disclosing the real state of the case, till the wretched man is on the steps. 'Where?' inquires the entrapped individual, with an attempt to back out again. 'Either side, Sir,' rejoins the cad, shoving him in, and slamming the door. 'All right, Bill.' Retreat is impossible; the new-comer rolls about, till he falls down somewhere, and there he stops.'

There is also a lively portrait of a Mr Barker who took up the profession of a cad on a bus and resolved to make it pay.

'Commend me to an omnibus'—Boz, *The Omnibus*

> His active mind at once perceived how much might be done in the way of enticing the youthful and unwary, and shoving the old and helpless into the wrong bus, and carrying them off, until reduced to despair, they ransomed themselves by the payment of sixpence a head, or, to adopt his own figurative expression in all its native beauty, 'till they was rig'larly done over, and forked out the stumpy.'

The passengers were sometimes so infuriated by the liberties taken by the cads that instead of 'forking out the stumpy' they reported them to the police and managed to get them sent to prison. As has already been said Boz wrote to entertain and we need not take too seriously every word that he said about the early London buses and their vigorous competition in collecting fare-payers for themselves and discouraging patronage of rivals. There was, he related, the practice of the driver of a second bus 'keeping constantly behind the first one and driving the pole of his vehicle either into the door of the other or through the body of any lady or gentleman who might make an attempt to get into it'. Mr Barker enjoyed that kind of cut-throat, or more precisely push-back, competition and enlivened it with a flow of Cockney banter.

That a conductor should be a man ready with his tongue and no respecter of self-important persons was a tradition long maintained. When women took over the work of conducting buses during the last war these 'clippies', as they were called, could hold their own in good Dickensian fashion. I remember being on a crowded bus during a rush-hour at that period when an air-vice-marshal of formidable aspect jostled ahead of the queue at a stopping-place and tried to get on. The clippy pushed him off and said to him, 'You get back, old cock, and mind your manners.' To this the old cock had no answer but a scowling obedience while a young naval officer, already on the bus, said to the girl, 'Good for you, ducks, I'll bring you an admiral for treatment tomorrow.' Dickens would have thought well of the clippy and the naval comment. He hated all bigwig and buzzfuzz pushers-forward and he enjoyed the pert back-answer. In this, by the infinite capacity for a 'come-back' which he bestowed on Sam Weller, he showed his own inventive skill in a matchless way.

Travel by cab is constant in the novels; the arrival of the railways banished the coaches but did not put the hackney carriage out of action. Dickens distinguished the hackney coach from the hackney cab. The former was an antiquated vehicle once belonging to a private family. A typical one is described as 'a great, lumbering, square concern of a dingy yellow colour (like a bilious brunette) with very small windows but very large frames; the panels are ornamented with a faded coat of arms'. It had two horses, also of a faded kind. To hire it was expensive since Parliament had fixed the fare for such contraptions at a shilling a mile. But despite the pair of horses its progress was stately, and was assessed by Boz (seventh *Sketch*) at four miles an hour.

The hackney cab, on the other hand, was born such and had no air of desolate grandeur; it covered, for eightpence a mile, at least six miles an hour and might even attain enough speed to be a menace. When Mr Pickwick was being driven to meet the Ipswich coach at the Bull Inn, Whitechapel, Mr Weller senior asked whether he was 'cabbin' it'. To this Sam replied, 'Yes, he's a-havin' two mile o' danger at eightpence.' Considering the purchasing power of money in the eighteen-thirties 'cabbin' it' seems a costly business. On the calculation that money then bought ten times what it can buy in the nineteen-sixties, as it certainly did in the way of food and some clothes, the hackney coach was hired at the equivalent of ten shillings a mile and the hackney cab at four.

The hansom cab reached the London streets in 1834 and stayed there for over eighty years. It was the invention of an architect, Joseph Aloysius Hansom. This was an elegant, two-wheeled, one-horse vehicle whose carriage was set well above the ground. At first the driver and its passenger sat side by side, with the former unsheltered and the latter roofed in. But the early model was abandoned in favour of the long-prevailing two-seater, with room for a third passenger if 'a little 'un'. The driver sat high up at the back, looking out over the roof. Piling baggage there would block his view of the street ahead; so travellers with luggage had to use the four-wheeled cab, known as 'a crawler' because it could not compete with the hansom's speed. It was also called 'a growler' because the driver was usually cantankerous. In a world which had no taximeters there was always argument about the distance covered and the fare due. A statutory list of the chief London distances from point to point was drawn up; but few could memorise it except in the case of a journey which they were constantly making. So there was ample opportunity for arguing the point.

Dickens wrote of a red hansom, driven by a remarkable character with an aggressive temper and a fine contempt for danger. 'Bump they comes agin' the post and out flies the fare like bricks.' Mounting and dismounting the hansom with two slender steps, if the horse was restive, was quite a piece of work. Boz had studied the problem closely and decided that for getting out the best way was to make the driver get down first and then throw oneself upon him; in the event of a long journey there was less need to worry about a graceful exit because 'the probability is that you will be shot lightly out before you have completed the third mile'.

For private carriages the gentry had the four-wheeled barouche, which was open, and the enclosed sociable, which had a dickey-seat or 'rumble' at its back; this was occupied by the footman. Others of this kind were the brougham, named after a famous Lord Chancellor, and the royally entitled victoria. There was also a light and rather dashing carriage called the phaeton. This was a curious choice of name since the Phaethon of ancient Greek mythology was a son of the Sun, who got his father's permission to drive the solar chariot across the sky. Shakespeare alluded to him as lacking 'the manage of unruly steeds', and according to the legend he could not control his horses, came too near the earth, singed it, and thus created the coloured races. For his blunder his pitiless father killed him with a flash of lightning. It was an ill-omened title for any vehicle, but the phaeton, as it came to be spelled without the second 'h', was no more perilous than a hansom cab and moved lightly and prettily in London's competition of dashing carriages.

The term 'chariot' for a carriage remained long in use and rattles through the novels of Dickens as it is found spanking through the stories and plays of the eighteenth century. We with our assortment of motor cars have a wide range of choice, but the mid-Victorian gentry when purchasing a private conveyance had a number of neat, lightly sprung, and delicately designed chariots of one kind or another from which to select. These would overtake the decaying timbers of the jogtrot hackney coach about which Boz was so sarcastic. But the hansom, a vehicle favoured by the upstart M.P., Mr Veneering of *Our Mutual Friend*, could rival them all in looks and speed and add to the gaiety of the town with the driver's back-chat and slangy conversation. The long-distance coaches had gone and their 'bugle-horns', as Dickens called them, no longer made music on the road, but the tradition of a driver with a tongue in his head as well as reins in his hands vivaciously continued.

CHAPTER SEVEN

Going by Train

THE railway trains in the novels of Dickens are tremendous and terrifying engines of the new mobility. 'Away once more into the day and through the day, with a shrill yell of exultation, and roaring, rattling, tearing on, spurning everything . . . shrieking, roaring, rattling through the purple distance. Louder and louder yet it shrieks and cries as it tears on resistless to its goal.'

What is this Juggernaut which is careering in a blaze of sparks and a cloud of smoke across the face of England? It is only the London to Birmingham train which is carrying Mr Dombey and Major Joey Bagstock on a visit to Leamington Spa. They are travelling in the gentlemanly style of their time. For their carriage has been lifted at the starting terminus on to an open truck, fixed there, and left for them to sit in and survey the scenery as the Juggernaut propels them on its way through a gap in the Chiltern Hills. On they are whirled in a tumult of din which, as the reader may notice, has moved the author to some repetition in his use of clatter-language.

We are so accustomed to the zooming of aeroplanes above us, the uproar of motor engines, the grinding of brakes, the changing of gears, and the honking in the streets of our cities that we are becoming comparatively noise-proof; indeed we must become so if we are not to find urban life completely unbearable. The impetus and rattle of an express train as we see and hear it hurtle through a small main-line station or go pelting past a level crossing in open country is an experience so common as to be little noticed. Even a sky as noisy as the earth is increasingly taken for granted.

The opening of the Hungerford Suspension Bridge, 1st May 1845

But we have to think ourselves back into a period in which the railway engine was just replacing the horse coach, and at one point had burst its way into London exactly where Dickens had lived and gone to his lessons at Wellington House in the Hampstead Road with no more rumpus about him than the clip-clop of a tradesman's pony. It was naturally a shock when the change came and the corner of London that he knew best was belching steam and smoke and making a raucous assault upon the unaccustomed ear.

The first entry of the trains had come elsewhere. The tiny London and Greenwich line was the pioneer when it ran to and from the first of the termini. Its London base was at London Bridge, opened in 1836, south of the river and so with no need for a railway bridge. Two years later, for the western line, there was a station at Paddington, but it was a small affair and nothing like the great building that was put in its place between 1850 and 1854. The south-western line had its first headquarters at Nine Elms, but there was a closer approach to the river at Waterloo in 1848. The fine reconstruction of that station that we know was only begun in 1907. The southern lines which crossed the river had of course to wait for the railway bridges to be built. Charing Cross got its bridge in 1860, a deplorably ugly one which has been an eyesore ever since and a hindrance to the right development of the South Bank. This replaced the graceful old Hungerford suspension bridge designed by Brunel and opened for road traffic in 1845. That piece of fine early-Victorian design was lost to London but not to England since it was removed to Clifton to cross the gorge of the Bristol Avon.

Charing Cross station followed the construction of the new unsightly bridge in 1864. Farther east another railway bridge made a second link between central London and the southern counties in the same year, when the City men could come in for business from the Kent suburbs to Cannon Street. To the west again there was a further entry at Victoria, which was first built as a humble place with wooden frontages for the little Victoria and Pimlico railway and then leased to the soon rapidly expanding London, Brighton, and South Coast and the London, Chatham, and Dover railways. We can see in the history of Charing Cross the enormous alterations during the lifetime of Dickens of a section of London indelibly impressed on his memory.

During his boyhood months in the Blacking Factory at Hungerford Stairs Scotland Yard was the name of a wharf where coal from barges was taken ashore. It had a labourers' village life of its own, which was richly described by Dickens in the fourth of the Boz *Sketches* with a drawing by George Cruikshank of the old public-house. Here 'the lusty coal-heavers' involved the room in clouds of tobacco smoke as they took their large draughts of beer round a huge open fire. They were mighty men for a chorus and a popular song and were especially vocal after they had eaten puddings and pies of enormous size and solidity in the two local eating-houses.

Soon the nearness to Whitehall and the offices of Government made the area too valuable to be left as a village. The Commissioners of Police came in and began to create the Scotland Yard of today, and the arrival of the developing Civil Service made the place truly urban and, for Dickens, dismally genteel. The new kind of Charing Cross was growing up but the old name lingered. The Scotland part of it was based on the previous existence of a palace which was used in the Middle Ages by the Kings of Scotland if they came to London to negotiate or pay fealty. The Yard was the docking-place of the coal barges. Now everybody has heard of Scotland Yard and few know the cause of its title or its condition, squalid perhaps but lively, when Dickens went to the hated labours of his boyhood.

When he was thirty-three and already more than a prosperous and famous man he saw the suspension bridge span the river and when he was forty-eight its replacement by the railway bridge. Five years after that the cross which we pass on entering and leaving the station was erected. This may look like a genuine antique, but it was a Victorian imitation of one of twelve crosses set up by Edward I in 1291 when the body of Queen Eleanor was brought for burial at Westminster. Here was the last halting-place of the funeral procession before it reached the Abbey. Thus the name of Charing Cross was a very old one, but the original cross was destroyed by the Puritans in 1643. It was the railway company that organised and paid for the new memorial to Edward's queen. So the innovation did in a way restore a feature of great antiquity.

Thus Dickens had seen on the spot where Dr Johnson descried 'the full tide of human existence' the sweeping flow of change. The Scotland Yard of his childhood was a relic of the eighteenth and earlier centuries, with barge and cart to provide the traffic. Before he died the trains were puffing out with their passengers for Chatham and Dover and the drinking-songs of the bargees were replaced by the scream and rattle of the new transport. There still remained till the day of his death the old Northumberland House, the last of the great medieval riverside mansions of the earls and dukes; this was pulled down in 1874 to make way for Northumberland Avenue and the new London of vast offices, hotels, and clubs. But its garden is mentioned by Boz as one of the boundaries of the old grimy and convivial Scotland Yard.

But Dickens did see in his last years the entire alteration of the north bank of the Thames when Sir Joseph Bazalgette started in 1864 to construct the great Victoria Embankment, penning in the river with a strong protecting wall and providing a broad convenient roadway from Westminster to the City in the place of the mud-flats previously exposed by the ebbing tides. Thus the big riverside termini of Victoria, Charing Cross, and Cannon Street were linked with a serviceable road and the traffic between the stations was not confined to the old and narrow Strand and Fleet Street.

But the part of the railway development which impressed him most was that of the northern lines. His work at Hungerford Stairs had not been a long incarceration. His boyhood in Camden Town had been an ampler and a happier spell, whatever he thought of the educational methods at Wellington House. Here he saw a whole region invaded and in process of a drastic social upheaval.

Not long ago the houses which looked in a north-westerly direction from the Euston Road were set back from the street with

Chalk Farm Bridge, the Birmingham Railway

a space in front of them. The space was planned as a garden in which the owners could sit on a pleasant day or evening and look across the fields and scattered villages of Camden Town, Somers Town, and Kentish Town to the wooded heights of Highgate and Hampstead. (This pleasant sight can still be seen from the top of a bus in the Tottenham Court Road.) Well into the nineteenth century that was the end of London and the beginning of a countryside once agreeably famous for 'peaches and snipe', but soon to be smutched with rubbish-heaps and cheap untidy buildings. Because the town had come to an end with the lordly town-planning of the Duke of Bedford's Bloomsbury estate, the northerly railways when they arrived had to end here. Hence the row of three great termini, Euston, St Pancras, and King's Cross.

Of these Euston came first. The making of a London to Birmingham railway was legalised by an Act passed as early as May 1833 but the track was to begin at Camden Town; an Act of July 1835 enabled the extension to Euston to be made. There were naturally many difficulties for the pioneers in tunnelling and the passage from Euston to Camden Town meant burrowing under the Hampstead Road and crossing the Regent's Canal. That took time. Moreover the gradient up to Chalk Farm, though it now seems slight enough to a road passenger going from Warren Street, was found difficult and so a stationary engine was placed at Camden Station. Trains in Euston were attached to this engine by a long cable which helped to haul them on their outward and upward way. The development of the line from London to Birmingham was an exactly Victorian creation since the section from Euston to Boxmoor was opened in July 1837, just after the accession of the young Queen. It was completed eleven months later. When Dickens was twenty-six he could have gone to Birmingham by train, but that kind of travel was still rather experimental. The Euston buildings of those years had none of the grandeur which was soon to come and to be completed in 1846. That was the year in which he wrote *Dombey and Son*, which may be called the most railway-minded of all his long books.

This new Euston was built in the classic style with the architect Philip Hardwick's great Doric arch to usher in the traveller as though he were approaching some capital city of ancient Greece with a temple instead of a terminus ahead of him. Behind it was a great central hall designed in the Roman style with a gallery running round it, a nobly panelled ceiling, and abundant painting and sculpture. The London to Birmingham traveller, though he arrived at Euston top-hatted in the manner of the day, could feel that he was being sent on his way with the circumstance proper to an Athenian philosopher or a Roman Emperor. His train might have to be pulled out of the station by a rope; but at least he had, as he took his ticket amid classic halls and chambers, the sense of starting on a triumphal procession.

The great arch could hardly be defended in later years on grounds of utility; it was deemed a nuisance and destroyed in the replanning of Euston in 1961. There were strong protests, all the stronger because Victorian tastes and achievements were no longer being regarded with the amused derision which had previously been the dismissive fashion. If the arch was 'a folly' it could be defended as a noble foolishness and an impressive effort to give massive dignity to the dominating power that lay in the new industry of mechanical transport. But its splendour was not allowed to counterbalance its irrelevance. So vanished the classic gateway through which Dickens must have driven many times in his later life when he took train to give the famous readings of his works, to speak at meetings, to visit the midlands and the north, to inspect the new industrial England and denounce the mess that was being made in that age of chimney-stacks and clattering machines. Dickens was obviously extremely sensitive to noise and resented the din as much as the drabness of the manufacturing towns, just as he winced at the uproar of the trains.

King's Cross, with a handsome frontage by Lewis Cubitt, was built in 1852. When Euston and King's Cross could no longer accommodate the northern and north-westerly traffic the vast Gothic pile of St Pancras was erected between them, a start being made in 1868 by Sir George Gilbert Scott in the romantic Victorian style which was to sprinkle turrets and towers over many parts of England and Scotland, not least in the Highland castles of the new Scottish lords of industry. So the passengers could leave London through a baronial mansion as well as by Euston's classic gateway. St Pancras, unfinished when Dickens died, soared to a clock-tower of three hundred feet. Matthew Arnold spoke of Oxford's dreaming spires; St Pancras, with the fume of its engines, had its steaming ones.

It is plain that the poor and squalid region known as Staggs's Gardens, where Florence Dombey's foster-mother, Polly Toodle, lived, was, as Dickens imagined it, situated where the new and imposing railway line from Euston was to run. It was a clearance which Dickens did not regret; he was never sentimental about the old if the old was an unhealthy sore on the body of a town. The Gardens were not unjustly named when the inhabitants could grow a row of beans and keep fowls round the sheds in which they lived. But the railway came 'like the first shock of a great earthquake'. Houses were knocked down and streets broken through. 'Carcases of ragged tenements were replaced by piles of scaffolding and a wilderness of brick.' Before long 'the miserable waste ground where the refuse-matter had been heaped of yore, was swallowed up and gone; and in its frowzy stead were tiers of warehouses, crammed with rich goods and costly merchandise.' Yet some of the housing behind Euston remained deplorable for a century or more.

However, in the bustle of those train-roaring forties the railway epoch had begun and Railway had become a popular and profitable trade-name. Dickens described the change in chapter 15 of *Dombey and Son*:

> As to the neighbourhood which had hesitated to acknowledge the railroad in its straggling days, that had grown wise and penitent, as any Christian might in such a case, and now boasted of its powerful and prosperous relation. There were railway patterns in its drapers' shops, and railway journals in the windows of its newsmen. There were railway hotels, coffee-houses, lodging-houses, boarding-houses; railway plans, maps, views, wrappers, bottles, sandwich-boxes, and time-tables; railway hackney-coach and cabstands; railway omnibuses, railway streets and buildings, railway hangers-on and parasites, and flatterers out of all calculation. There was even railway time observed in clocks,

> as if the sun itself had given in. Among the vanquished was the master chimney-sweeper, whilom incredulous at Staggs's Gardens, who now lived in a stuccoed house three stories high, and gave himself out, with golden flourishes upon a varnished board, as contractor for the cleansing of railway chimneys by machinery.

There was a new way of life and promotions came with it. Mr Toodle, newly housed, since Staggs's had gone, in one of the railway-company buildings, became proudly an engine fireman and then an engine driver. But the monster still had its menace for Dickens. In this same tale of the Dombeys the scoundrel Carker was caught by an express. There is a gruesome description of his end: 'beaten down, caught up and whirled away upon a jagged mill that spun him round and round and struck him limb from limb and licked his stream of life up with its fiery heat and cast his mutilated fragments in the air'.

Dickens himself was involved in a very serious railway accident in 1865. He was returning from a visit to France and coming to London by train from Folkestone harbour. At Staplehurst the train jumped a gap in a line on which men were working and eight coaches hurtled down a steep bank. A number of passengers were killed and more injured. Dickens, luckily unhurt, was able to take part in the rescue work; he carried brandy with him on his journeys and he administered his supply perhaps too generously, not knowing that alcohol is now deemed inadvisable in cases of shock. He was later given a presentation of plate by the company for his good work in that disaster, from which he never wholly recovered his nerve. The monster, of whose seeming ferocity he had written twenty years before, had lived up to his apprehensive picture of a Juggernaut.

Mugby Junction was written in 1866, the year after the Staplehurst crash. A man is killed in this tale, cut down by an engine; but the interest as far as the railway service is concerned lies in the development of the tracks and multiplication of trains during the twenty years since *Dombey and Son* was written. Mugby, which may or not be associated with Victorian Rugby and might be a memory of Crewe, although remote from a big city, has woven a vast network of lines:

> A place replete with shadowy shapes, this Mugby Junction in the black hours of the four-and-twenty. Mysterious goods trains, covered with palls and gliding on like vast weird funerals, conveying themselves guiltily away from the presence of the few lighted lamps, as if their freight had come to a secret and unlawful end. Half-miles of coal pursuing in a Detective manner, following when they lead, stopping when they stop, backing when they back. Red-hot embers showering out upon the ground, down this dark avenue, and down the other, as if torturing fires were being raked clear; concurrently, shrieks and groans and grinds invading the ear, as if the tortured were at the height of their suffering. Iron-barred cages full of cattle, jangling by mid-way, the drooping beasts with horns entangled, eyes frozen with terror, and mouths too: at least they have long icicles (or what seem so) hanging from their lips. Unknown languages in the air, conspiring in red, green, and white characters. An earthquake, accompanied with thunder and lightning, going up express to London.

At night there was no pause or respite from the din which always seemed to torment Dickens when he was in a train or beside a track.

In another random tale which appeared in the same volume as *Mugby Junction*, *The Lazy Tour of Two Idle Apprentices*, there is a similar picture of a large junction in the country; this time we are in Cumberland but not in the city of Carlisle:

> All manner of cross-lines came zig-zagging out of it like a Congress of iron vipers . . . sidings were there in which empty luggage-vans and

> cattle-boxes butted against each other as if they could not agree: and ware-houses were there in which great quantities of goods seemed to have taken the veil (in the consistency of tarpaulin) and to have retired from the world without any hope of getting back to it.

And of course there was the gloomy refreshment room, where nobody with any palate could possibly be refreshed. The coaches and the horses, the music of the horn, and the drawing up at an inn with steaming jugs and bowls for the shivering and huge sirloins for the hungry are already part of a lost world. There was none of the welcome, none of the cordial acceptance of an open house, for the traveller who had to change trains and wait an hour or two at Mugby Junction.

Yet, although this spread of tracks and stations had been rapid, England, with all its new engineering resources, had lagged behind the young America. It must puzzle the readers of *Martin Chuzzlewit*, written in 1843 about English life of a slightly earlier period, to find that a journey from Salisbury to London had to be made by coach and that Martin, when he had crossed the Atlantic, could travel on a railway. The engine of his train had three great caravans or cars attached, 'the ladies' car, the gentlemen's car, and the car for negroes'. The track had been badly laid, the bumps and jerks were frightful, and so was the noise. But Dickens, while deriding the Americans of the time for many of their pretensions and their canting eloquence about their Free New World, could not deny that the nation so ready with its tongue had also been ready with its railway engineers and had got ahead with the communications of the new age. It could be claimed for Britain that many of the first locomotives had been imported by the Americans from there. One, the 'Stourbridge Lion', made its first run in America in 1829, the year in which the Stephensons won a prize for their 'Rocket'.

THE RAILWAY—FIRST CLASS.

(Continued from page 325.)
crease, concludes the reader. Alas! for the *hosts* who could testify far otherwise. At the head-quarters of resort in the town of Epsom—where whilom, during the meeting week, you might as well have sought for a bed for yourself or a stall for your horse, as for that *lusus naturæ* that Diogenes looked for with his lantern—only one guest slept the night before the Derby, and three horses constituted the cavalry department! But what of that?

"Tempora mutantur nos et mutamur in illis."

SECOND CLASS.

The Railway—first class, second class and third class

The Americans were well ahead also in matters of comfort. They used the big open saloons instead of small compartments and before *Mugby Junction* was written these had air-conditioning of a kind, with the air passed through cold water for hot weather and proper heating by hot air for winter. For forty or fifty years the English railway traveller in cold weather had to get his warmth from large metal hot-water bottles put on the floor of his carriage when the train started.

As foot-rests these did serve to thaw cold feet and they also helped to create a general frowst, sufficient to make the journey endurable for those who preferred a fug to a freeze. On long trips, say from London to Scotland, the cans would be noisily exchanged for newly heated ones when the train stopped at York. It was a primitive way of coping with a problem which the Americans had solved much earlier.

On the American railways there was a colour-bar, on the British a money-bar. The social distinctions, based on capacity to pay, were rigid. The wealthy sat in the first class, travelling with their servants placed in the second class. The others went in third-class carriages which were little better than cattle-trucks with the addition of rough roofs and windows; no cushions were there, and according to the pictures in the illustrated and comic papers of the time no luggage-racks, nothing but bare boards. In none of the classes was smoking permitted during the first thirty years of railway travel, but the rule was apt to be broken with a tip to the guard to ease the latter's oversight. Later on it became compulsory to have some smoking accommodation on every train. Another enactment at Westminster created 'the Parliamentary train'. On all lines, large or small, there had to be at least one train a day in each direction carrying third-class passengers at a fare not exceeding a penny a mile. These Parliamentaries could be as slow and uncomfortable as the railway companies liked; they catered for the poor and were kept standing about while the rich man's express rolled by. But the expresses were no models of amenity by our standards either. The lighting came from an oil-lamp let down through the roof. At Mugby Junction there was a railway-man known as 'Lamps' who used to skip along the top of the carriages of a waiting train and insert the lighted lamps passed up to him by a colleague. 'Lamps' had a special room where he trimmed and fed his wicks with oil and got ready for his roof-skipping when a train needed to be serviced in this way. If the travellers wanted to sleep they could pull a cloth cover over the light inserted above them.

It was long before even the first-class passengers had a chance of physical relief without getting out at a station where their expresses stopped. But in the years just before his death Dickens could take his place in a family or saloon car which had seats set round as in a room. There was next to it a second-class compartment for servants and a water-closet. John Gloag in his book on *Victorian Comfort* describes the plight of those who had not been accommodated in the new saloon coaches:

> The lack of this convenience on ordinary long-distance trains caused excessive discomfort, and although some rather odd appliances for the relief of travellers could be bought, it was impossible for ladies to ask for such things, even if they had known about them. When ladies travelled together in a compartment, as they generally preferred to, they were able to include in their luggage an innocent-looking circular basket, which contained a chamber pot. When sleeping cars were first put into service early in the '70's, on the North British and London and North Western long-distance trains, water closets were provided; but it was not until the Great Western built the first corridor coaches in 1892 that all classes of passengers had access to them.

This is not a subject which Dickens cares to mention. He was very prim in such matters. The plumbing and even the washing accommodation available for his characters are not mentioned, though we should naturally be interested to know how they managed in these affairs.

As the history of the railways advanced the companies found it necessary to attract the poorer members of the public by advertising excursion tickets. At Easter 1862, for example, the people of Leeds were invited to spend a holiday in London for a return fare of ten shillings, the total distance covered being three hundred and forty miles. The Parliamentary fare for that at a penny a mile would have been twenty-eight shillings and sixpence. So there were bargains to be had, but those enjoying them financially suffered for them bodily.

During the last decade of Dickens's life the monster became a mole or rather a dragon working underground and spewing smoke and sparks. The Metropolitan Railway Company was founded in 1854 to cope with London's rapidly growing transport problem by providing lines beneath the roads. There were serious difficulties to be faced, not only of an engineering kind. Many feared that the tunnelling just below the streets and houses would endanger their property and the company was immediately met with a flood of compensation claims.

The first route selected for subterranean travel in London was from Bishop's Road, Paddington, to Farringdon Street, linking the western and northern termini. Nine years elapsed between the formation of the company and the first journey along the line in 1863. There had been serious interruptions of the work, which had none of the modern tunnelling apparatus and had to be carried out by the manual labour of the navvies. One of the principal nuisances was the continued existence in sewer form of London's buried rivers, the largest of which, the Fleet, ran down from Hampstead Heath to the Thames by way of Clerkenwell and Farringdon Street. For centuries it had been in places an open water-course vilely misused as a drain and as a receptacle for offal and filth of all kinds. The poet Pope had written a century before the childhood of Dickens of the scene at what is now Ludgate Circus:

> Where Fleet with disemboguing streams
> Rolls the large tribute of dead dogs to Thames.
> The King of Dykes! Than whom no sluice of mud
> With deeper sable blots the silver flood.

The Fleet was later entirely covered in and became a useful conduit, as it still is. But when there was heavy rain in north London the rush of waters was turned into a torrent and broke out of its confining tunnel. (It continued to be a menace to the sewer-men, but they are now given good warning and can make for safety when, after a downpour, the Fleet sewer is filled with a swirling cataract.) In 1862, just when the new Underground was nearing completion, there was a dangerous outbreak of waters in the Clerkenwell section and further delays.

But in January 1863 parties of Very Important Persons were given trial runs over the new railway. Mr Gladstone, then Chancellor of the Exchequer, and his wife were passengers on one occasion, sitting in an open truck as the train clattered triumphantly on its way under an astonished London. The use of open trucks on that day did not mean that the new service was to be a crude one. Indeed, the carriages put into use were better designed and more comfortable than those on the main-line railways. The class distinctions were strictly maintained and the labels First, Second, and Third applied to refreshment rooms and waiting-rooms as well as to the train compartments. The carriages were lit with gas and did not need the constant attentions of Mugby Junction's 'Lamps'. Despite the pestilential smoke and consequent dirt the Underground lines were popular, profitable, and rapidly extended. Before

Gladstone at Edgware Road Station on 24th May 1862, during the trial trip of the Metropolitan Railway

Dickens died the 'Met' was circling its way by way of Kensington to Sloane Square and Westminster.

At Sloane Square there was another 'buried river' difficulty, since the line had here to cope with the Tyburn stream. But this was not so large or dangerous as the Fleet and could be disciplined. Passengers at Sloane Square Station today can still see the great pipe which carries the Tyburn over their heads and over the trains. There were cries of alarm when the Underground approached Westminster. Would not the Abbey collapse? The engineers could cope with that and Dickens was buried there in 1870 with none doubting that his grave would remain in position and not sink into a chaos of collapsed tunnels, where the Juggernaut of his boyhood was now rumbling smokily but safely along.

CHAPTER EIGHT

Bed and Board

THE epoch of the Grand Hotel in the centre of the town was yet to come; on the seaside promenade it was just beginning. The railways helped to introduce it. The age of the coaches demanded chiefly a well-distributed supply of inns set along the roads at the various stages, where horses were changed, thirsts were quenched in summer, and bodies were defrosted in winter. The travellers were not settling in for a stay; they were there for the night, like many of the coach parties who tour Britain nowadays, of course with much greater speed, being carried to and from the south and round the Scottish Highlands in a fortnight or less.

In the country towns the principal inn was not only a recipient of the passers-by: it was a place for local celebrations and hospitalities. It is noticeable that the inns surviving from the eighteenth and early nineteenth centuries beside the old market-places often have a large and elegant room for an assembly or a dance as well as the dining-room and a 'snug' with an atmosphere of cosy mustiness for conversational drinking and the mustering of cronies. Long stays for a country holiday were not expected. Taking holidays away from home in country places is a fairly recent habit which began with the development of fashionable spas and health resorts for wealthy people. One of these was Leamington, visited by Mr Dombey and Major Joey Bagstock, who took rooms at the Royal Hotel.

Even in those places going to hotels was not general. Mrs Skewton and her daughter, the future Mrs Dombey, were in lodgings and these lodgings were commodious and well staffed.

They had the attention of a page-boy, which nobody would now expect in 'digs'. Genteel families, when they were away from home, looked for what Jane Austen called 'accommodations', a term which used to live on in placards set in landladies' windows but is now rarely seen. When the Elliots in her novel *Persuasion* left Kellynch to visit Bath, Sir Walter, as befitted 'a man who never took up any book but the Baronetage', rented a house; he did not take his girls to an hotel. It was 'a very good house in Camden Place, a lofty dignified situation, such as becomes a man of consequence'. But his friend, Lady Russell, took lodgings. We now associate 'digs' with students and those who cannot pay much. But then lodgings could be deemed socially correct for people of title.

Persuasion was finished in 1816; it just overlaps the childhood of Dickens. But many of the customs of the Regency period survived through late Georgian into Victorian times. As was said, it was the coming of railway travel that took away the trade of the roadside inns and made necessary a new kind of hotel near the station. Some were of a grandiose and expensive type catering for important people and others dingy and cheap to suit the purses of minor commercial travellers. Gradually hotels of all grades in holiday resorts became general, but when Dickens's Tuggs family went to Ramsgate for a long stay in summer they did not mention going to an hotel. They took lodgings. There was no fear of overcrowding then, no booking well ahead. On arrival by steamer they hired a 'fly' and drove round the town until they found 'a dusty house with a bay-window, from which you could thrust half your body out of it, at the imminent peril of falling into the area'. One ground-floor sitting-room and three small bedrooms were taken. The rent with attendance, which meant 'the privilege of ringing the bell as often as you like for your amusement', was five guineas a week. Considering that money then was many times more

Plymouth Public Library

valuable than it is today this seems a stiff price. Nothing is said about board. But the shrimps brought in for tea were voted capital after Mr Tuggs senior had been well scolded by his family for calling them 'srimps', a London habit of long duration.

The Tuggs family holiday is worth noticing as a specimen of middle-class life in the eighteen-thirties as it was enjoyed in seaside 'accommodations'. For six weeks the routine of leisured gaiety was observed: 'Sands in the morning, donkeys at noon, pier in the afternoon, library at night.' The library was not so literary as it sounds. There gathered 'the same ladies and the same gentlemen who had been on the sands in the morning and on the pier the day before'. There were marriageable daughters and marriage-making mammas playing games of chance and there were male beaux 'doing the sentimental in whispers and others doing the ferocious in moustaches'. The gentlemen wore braided coats, gilt waistcoats, and shirt-frills. It was quite a cavalcade of bourgeois fashion that set out from the lodgings in the evenings to sample the pleasures of the library, where further entertainment was laid on. 'Mrs Tippin "of the London theatres" sang the popular cavatina of "Bid me Discourse", accompanied at the piano by Mr Tippin.' After that Mr Tippin sang a comic song and Miss Tippin played the guitar.

Ramsgate was obviously catering for the simple folk of moderate means. Brighton had more 'class' and many hotels. It was full of those who had been 'ordered sea-air'. The railways made it 'London by the sea' and it was later to become almost a suburb. Mr Dombey, in the railway age, could get down quickly to visit Paul and Florence and stayed at an hotel, which is named the Bedford, while Major Bagstock was at another, not named and presumably less expensive. The children were established, or perhaps one should say incarcerated, at the house or 'castle' of Mrs Pipchin, a formidable widow who kept what Mrs Tox described as 'an infantine boarding-house of a very select description'. It had half a dozen specimens of cactus writhing in a flinty garden and was prolific in earwigs. A very little teaching was given between meals, which were mainly farinaceous for the 'infantine' guests and greasy and fleshy for Mrs Pipchin, who had a powerful appetite for hot buttered toast and chops. Poor Florence stayed on there when Paul was removed to Dr Blimber's academy.

Dickens, with his middle-class origin and Kentish loyalty, was much kinder to Ramsgate than he was to Brighton. But even in his most sombre books, of which *Dombey and Son* is certainly one, he wrote intermittently to amuse and Mrs Pipchin's establishment is brilliantly ridiculed. Boarding-houses then accepted that name and had keepers. They had not become guest-houses with hostesses and romantically geographical names like Balmoral or Killarney.

Mrs Pipchin's floral taste was for the cactus, which has become oddly fashionable, and not for the aspidistra, which has become a joke.

Boarding-houses were popular in towns for the accommodation of commercial gentlemen. The finest Dickensian specimen is Todgers's in the City, which had a large number of 'permanents', young bachelors in the lower grades of business. It had rooms for occasional visitors from the country and was thus patronised by Mr Pecksniff and his daughters. Todgers's was pictured as lying behind the river wharves in a medley of fruit-stores and decayed churches. It was so buried in tall buildings and alleys and by-ways that strangers had to be guided there; no verbal direction was of any use. It smelled incessantly of boiled cabbage 'as if all the greens that were ever boiled there were evergreens and flourished in immortal strength. It had not been papered or painted, hadn't Todgers's, within the memory of man.' But the commercial gentlemen stayed on and did themselves quite handsomely despite the stench from the kitchen and the further odour of rats and mice. They began the day solidly since there was a huge round of cold boiled beef on the table. Mrs Todgers must have cooked to satisfaction although she relieved their dishes of some of their best before they reached the boarders. Her method with a stew, as described by Benjamin, the perky, irrepressible boy servant, was 'dodging among the tender pieces with a fork and eating of them'.

At any rate Todgers's could rise to it. When the gentlemen boarders insisted on entertaining the Pecksniffs, more for the sake of the daughters than of the father, the Sunday dinner, served at five o'clock, was impressive. The table was 'groaning with boiled beef, roast veal, bacon, and pies' as well as with cakes and puddings of special preparation. 'Besides which there were bottles of stout, bottles of wine, bottles of ale and divers other strong drinks, native and foreign', the consumption of which encouraged Mr Pecksniff, before complete physical collapse, to exclaim to his fellow-diners, 'Let us be moral. Let us contemplate existence.' So, though Todgers's was as melancholy in structure and had as little fresh air as a tomb, it became a house of victuals and vivacity when the commercial gentlemen were having a Sunday spree.

Hotels in the City were then favoured by the kind of country visitors who would now go to Kensington, Bloomsbury, or Bayswater. When Charlotte and Anne Brontë undertook the great adventure of coming to London and explaining to their publishers the secret of the pseudonyms which the sisters had been using, Currer, Ellis, and Acton Bell, they stayed at the Chapter Coffee House in Paternoster Row. They were here close to St Paul's and not far from Dickens's imaginary, but probably fairly actual, Todgers's. Mrs Gaskell in her *Life of Charlotte Brontë* gives a picture of this hotel as she found it later when empty and deserted.

It seemed to be two hundred years old, and had low ceilings with heavy beams. In the eighteenth century it had been the resort of booksellers, publishers, and literary hacks, critics, and even wits in search of ideas or employment. Later it became 'the tavern frequented by University men and country clergymen who were up in London for a few days and, having no private funds or access into society, were glad to learn what was going on in the world of letters from the conversation which they were sure to hear in the Coffee-room'. Mr Brontë had taken his daughters there when he was convoying them to Brussels, but it was, added Mrs Gaskell, mainly a masculine resort and it was a strange place for the Miss Brontës to have chosen. However, 'a grey-haired, elderly waiter was touched by the great simplicity of these strangers and did all he could to make them feel at home'. They evidently appreciated this since they refused their publishers' hospitality and stayed on at the Chapter House.

Charlotte found it not only kindly but enlivening. She preferred the City to the West End. The former seemed 'so much more in earnest', she said. 'The City is getting its living, the West End but enjoying the pleasures. At the West End you may be amused. But in the City you are deeply excited.' At a neighbouring house of the Todgers's type the sisters might have been both amused, excited, and a little alarmed. But probably ladies did not go unescorted to boarding-houses for commercial gentlemen.

In 1828, nearly twenty years before the Brontë visit, Dickens was working as a reporter in the Consistory Court of Doctors' Commons, whose archaic procedure both amused and annoyed him. It lay on the south side of St Paul's and thus was close to the Chapter Coffee House whose literary life could have attracted him. But the country clergymen may have deterred him from being a caller for refreshment. Near by also were all the old taverns adjacent to Todgers's. They were the resort of grumbling wheezy old codgers who were yet marvellously long-winded in their gasping way. 'They were much opposed to steam and all newfangled ways and held ballooning to be sinful' and most of them believed that virtue went out with hair-powder and that Old England's greatness had decayed with barbers. Dickens had obviously penetrated this cluster of inns, the patrons of whose dimly-lit parlours could, as he said, 'fill a goodly book'. As it is they fill a goodly paragraph, and Todgers's, whose original he must have explored, fills more than that. There were more rewarding hours for the coming essayist and novelist of London life available among these malt-worms than among the rural vicars and bookish gossips of the Chapter Coffee House.

The Brontës had an all-night journey sitting up in the train from Keighley and on reaching their hotel in the morning they naturally 'refreshed themselves with washing'. But they did not lie and bask in a hot bath. These joys had not yet come. Hotel bedrooms were equipped with large washstand, marble-topped and ready with ample china from ewer and basin to chamber-pot. There is not much washing in Dickens, and baths, when taken, meant sponging in a hip-bath in front of the fire. Bathrooms came very slowly into London life. There were servants enough to carry large jugs of hot water up countless stairs, and the poor, if and when they washed all over, would do so by the kitchen fire.

Shower-baths were introduced before the kind of baths in which we lie and relax among the steam. But it was not until well after

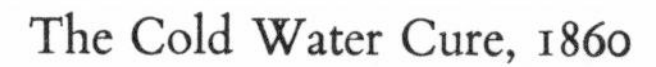

The Cold Water Cure, 1860

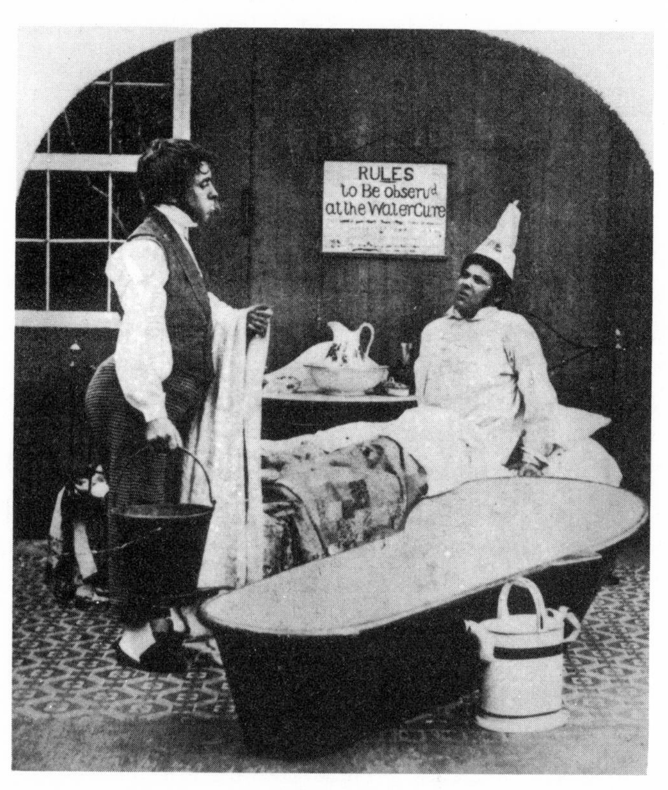

the death of Dickens that bathrooms as we know them became general even in prosperous households. Closely investigating the lives of Sherlock Holmes and Dr Watson at 221A Baker Street is a sport which I have practised along with many others, and I have paid special attention to the washing facilities available. Almost nothing is said of the couple taking baths although they often returned from adventures as grimy as arduous, scrambling over roofs or having a midnight run of two miles across Hampstead Heath in their escape from the home of Charles Augustus Milverton, 'the worst man in London' and a character who might have threaded his nefarious way through the darkest thickets of a Dickens plot.

Holmes and Watson went to Baker Street for their lodgings, and the landlady, Mrs Hudson, with the aid of her staff including Billy the page, looked after them admirably although she had much to endure, including constant violin-playing, intermittent indoor pistol-practice, and the arrival on her doorstep of criminal and murderous characters and of a swarm of 'street arabs', the Baker Street Irregulars. The houses in the street, which was in a fashionable part of the town and named after Sir Edward Baker, who helped to develop the Portman Estate, were built between 1785 and 1800 and no bathroom would be put in then. We do not hear of housing reforms made by Mrs Hudson and I surmise that on the one occasion when there is news of a bath taken it was a fireside squat with the carriage of hot water from the basement. But about the end of the Holmes-Watson tenancy something must have been done. Bathrooms were becoming a general innovation in good houses.

A tub was the kind of washing that Dickens knew. How frequently it was taken is uncertain but it was accepted as satisfactory. One has a feeling that at establishments such as Todgers's even that kind of partial immersion was hardly known at all. The pert

Benjamin had plenty to do with his cleaning of boots and knives and pantry work without having to cart large cans of water upstairs. What he would have said if told to do so only the genius of Dickens for Cockney repartee could have invented. Yet, after a long day in the wet and windy top of a coach, what a blessing would have been a good long boil in a full-length bath! Hot liquors within the body would have been much assisted in defeating shivers and rheumatic pains with the presence of even hotter water outside and around the limbs.

It is sometimes said that we now soak ourselves too much and that it does us no good to be constantly scouring the skin. However, we enjoy it and our health and expectation of life are considerably better than those of the Dickensians. As to what are now called 'toilet' facilities, Dickens, a man with many taboos who would even call trousers 'unmentionables', naturally said nothing. Even now novelists do not as a rule go into details of plumbing in describing the homes or 'digs' of their characters, and Dickens, with his strict censorship on certain topics, would have been the last to let us know about the sanitation of his cosy taverns or of such city warrens as Todgers's. It is not a savoury matter for speculation. The earth-closet was long common in proletarian London.

The novels of Dickens began with the meandering humours of the Pickwick Club, humours which meant the taking of coaches and hiring of chaises and staying at inns as far apart as Ipswich and Tewkesbury. There are so many overnight stops in this and other tales that any comprehensive survey of the subject would need a book in itself. The houses of call are, on the whole, given the author's blessing; the service was willing, the food and drink abundant, and the clock was never allowed to be the tyrant of tavern and hotel life that it later became. If ringing the bell was a vain amusement in Ramsgate lodgings it worked well enough at any hour in most of the inns. It must be remembered that Dickens was no prod-nose housewife who looks under the bed for neglected sweepings and searches every cranny for dust. The victuals satisfied a masculine clientèle whose members were usually well anaesthetised with alcohol before they got to table. It was not the travellers' business to peep inside the kitchen and see what went on there and whether the staff washed their hands. It was not a world of refrigerators, white jackets, scrupulous managers, and sanitary inspectors. None the less, one hears of less food-poisoning than appears to be suffered in our more exacting times.

Even in ordinary urban taverns there was a general will to help. When Sam Weller, turned amorous and even poetical to the great distress of his father, wanted to write a 'walentine', he did so at the Blue Boar near Leadenhall market. There he had the freedom of the little parlour with a fire in which to set to work as a bard. For inspiration there was ninepennyworth of 'brandy-and-water luke' as well as the beauty of the lady. (The greeting-card which he was inscribing cost one shilling and sixpence, which seems an enormous price for the eighteen-thirties.) Inns on the road had 'commercial rooms', which are presented as rather bleak and frowsty with stale tobacco smoke, but they were populated by men in good heart and of plentiful invention. The company was ready to receive and to enjoy some of those quite long stories, with which Dickens interspersed *Pickwick* and which he discharged in other places too. To most of us now they are not so enjoyable and we are inclined to skip them, eager for the main narrative to start again.

The men of the period were great consumers of breakfast. We need not rely upon Dickens alone for information about a grand morning spread. The hunting men in the Surtees tales can be counted out; they were stoking up for a long day in the open. Peacock's master of conversation at Crotchet Castle, the Rev. Dr Folliott, affords better evidence of what sedentary folk might expect. In his opinion

A man of taste is seen at once in the array of his breakfast table. . . . chocolate, coffee, tea, cream, ham, eggs, tongue, cold fowl, all these are good and bespeak good knowledge in him who sets them forth; but the touchstone is fish. Anchovy is the first step, prawns and shrimps the second and I laud him who reaches to these; potted char and lampreys are the third, and a fine stretch of progression. But lobster is indeed matter for a May morning and demands a rare combination of knowledge and of virtue in him who sets it forth.

When Dickens went to Yorkshire with Hablot Browne in 1838 on the track of Mr Squeers he told in a letter to his wife of the meals provided at Greta Bridge, ten miles from Bowes, where the infamous school was to be found. It was the end of January and they arrived after a drive through snow at about eleven at night. It was fearfully cold and Dickens was in an agony of apprehension since there seemed to be nobody about in the inn.

Dinner down the River, 1862

But to our great joy we discovered a comfortable room with drawn curtains and a most blazing fire and in half an hour they gave us a smoking supper and a bottle of mulled port (in which we drank your health) and then we retired to a couple of capital bedrooms in each of which there was a rousing fire half way up the chimney. We have had for breakfast toast, cakes, a Yorkshire pie, a piece of beef about the size and shape of my portmanteau, tea, coffee, ham and eggs.

No trifling with a sliver of toast and some fruit juice! Of course we cannot tell how much of the food described in the Dickens meals was actually eaten, but the extent of the catering could be so lavish as to seem grotesque and gargantuan to us. It was not only at the banquets of rich men intent upon display such as Mr Veneering that course was added to course. When David Copperfield had been bought into the legal firm of Spenlow and Jorkins by his generous aunt and was set up in rooms in Buckingham Street, Adelphi, he decided to entertain Steerforth and two other young men to dinner. After consultation with his landlady, Mrs Crupp, and subsequent shopping, the menu was oysters, mock turtle soup, a pair of hot roast fowls, a dish of stewed beef with vegetables, 'two little corner things, as a raised pie and a dish of kidneys', tart and a jelly, cheese and celery, and then dessert. Mrs Crupp, who was no glutton for work, limited her cooking to the potatoes; the other dishes were sent in from a cook-shop. For four the dinner should certainly have sufficed. David's ensuing collapse was not attributed to overeating. The wines had matched the victuals in abundance.

It was taken for granted in the eighteenth and nineteenth centuries that poultry was an inconsiderable kickshaw and must be accompanied by a joint or several dishes of butcher's meat to make a dinner that would not be a disgrace. Parson Woodforde kept in his diary a full record of the eating that went on in his

Norfolk vicarage and the amount consumed was enormous. His wife took for dinner one midday 'Some boiled beef rather fat and salt, a good deal of nice roast duck, and plenty of boiled damson pudding.' This she followed with plums, figs, and raspberries and cream. As a result 'she had a pain within her, blown up as if poisoned, attending with a vomiting'. She was dosed with rhubarb and ginger and was much better before she went to bed. The Parson added, 'I hope she will be brave to-morrow' and she proved brave enough to set about roast mutton.

The Woodforde statistics of consumption were astounding. When fourteen of the clergy got together after church and 'a very good sermon against Dissenters and Atheists', that reverend team sat down to cod, sirloin of beef roasted, leg of mutton boiled, pigeon pie, a roast goose and a couple of roast ducks, with plum and plain puddings boiled and plum and apple pies and dessert. For this each paid three shillings. That was well before Dickens's time, but there is no reason to suppose that the catering diminished and appetites dwindled. Victorian and Edwardian banquets continued to be enormously long, running to twelve courses separated half-way through by a sorbet or water-ice, which was taken to cleanse a sticky palate and create readiness for more.

Such feasting was not only occasional or limited to very rich folk. Dickens's contemporary, Thackeray, writing of his own middle class, complained of the monotony as well as the size of the entertainment given in family homes like his own: 'Everybody has the same dinner in London, the same soup, saddle of mutton, boiled fowls, tongue and other entrées.' The selection of entrées was numerous. It must be said on behalf of our seemingly gluttonous ancestors that they did not eat as often as we do. If they dined early, say between five and seven, as was usual, they cannot have done much feeding at midday. There was no snack-eating with cocktails and nibblings of biscuits with morning coffee and continual cups of tea. But when they settled down to a meal it was a meal, and it lasted a long time. When the poor had money and occasion for a spree they too could lay in. It was during the Christmas dinner at the humble home of Joe Gargery, the blacksmith in *Great Expectations*, that Uncle Pumblechook reverted to meat after the plum pudding and evoked from Mr Hubble the optimistic remark that 'a bit of savoury pork pie could lie atop of anything you could mention and do no harm'. The food-rationing of two wars compelled us to eat sparsely. It also taught us that we are better without whole series of meat dishes and that fowls, ducks, and geese are not trifles to be served as so much flummery after the joints of meat. Also, the cost of living has been another cause of more sensible feeding and a strong argument for abandoning the old habit of 'digging one's grave with one's teeth'. It is likely that many Victorians ate themselves if not to death at least well on the road to it, more perhaps than destroyed themselves with drinking.

There is a great deal of drinking in the novels of Dickens and some complain that there is too much of it. But there is no reason to suppose that his pictures of what Robert Burns called 'the social glass' in the tavern and of the private bottle in the home were much exaggerated. Alcoholic liquors were cheap, inns abounded, and here was an obvious consolation for the squalor and privations of the poor. For those who preferred it there was tea and that was universally and abundantly taken. In *The Pickwick Papers* (chapter 33) there is a famous description of tea consumption at the Brick Lane branch of the United Grand Junction Ebenezer Temperance Association, where the two Wellers, no addicts of the herb, watched the absorption. Mr Weller senior remarked, 'If some o' these here people don't want tappin' tomorrow mornin', I ain't your father, and that's wot it is. . . . There's a young 'ooman, on the next form but two, as has drunk nine breakfast cups and a half, and she's a-swellin' wisibly before my wery eyes.'

Tea had been introduced to England in 1657, and despite high taxation and high prices, which made it much more costly than gin-and-water, it had become enormously popular. An observer of London habits in 1797 said that even in the poor families tea was the usual beverage in the morning and evening and despite the price was also taken in large quantities with dinner. Parson Woodforde bought smuggled tea (with no shame at law-breaking) for ten shillings and sixpence a pound, a staggering price when one considers that he only paid three shillings for his share of a huge meal of many courses.

Dean Swift had called tea 'water bewitched' and there was general eagerness to partake of its charm. Until 1839 all the tea came from China; then importation from Assam began and the stronger and cheaper Indian teas captured the popular market. But since *The Pickwick Papers* were written some years before that, the imbibers at Brick Lane were drinking what was sometimes called Twankai after one of its Chinese sources. Those puzzled by the appearance of a comic dame called the Widow Twanky in the pantomime versions of the Aladdin story have their explanation in the name of Twankai. A Twanky was a 'tea-soak'. Our word 'tea' comes from the Chinese 'tcha' and this was turned into 'char' in soldiers' slang. So the cup of char now so commonly mentioned and absorbed should be China tea, but is nearly always the darker and more powerful brew of the Indian leaf, a fluid which, when left to stew, can merit the vulgar description of 'stomach stain'.

Beer or porter was a poor man's drink but it was preferred in a strengthened and heated form with spirits added. One of the varieties much appreciated was called 'Dog's Nose', which the secretary of the Brick Lane Ebenezers had discovered to be 'compounded of warm porter, moist sugar, gin and nutmeg'. The riverside workers who gathered at the Six Jolly Fellowship Porters, described in *Our Mutual Friend*, had a taste for similar mixtures called Flip and Purl as well as Dog's Nose. The inn, so sternly presided over by Miss Potterson, who allowed no drunkenness and firmly commanded the departure of those who had had enough, equipped her cosy bar with 'fireside tin-utensils, like models of sugar-loaf hats, made in that shape that they might with their pointed end seek out for themselves glowing nooks in the depths of the red coals, when they mulled your ale or heated those delectable drinks, Purl, Flip and Dog's Nose'. The addition to the basic beer or porter was usually gin and sometimes rum.

Admittedly the belief that 'work is the ruin of the drinking classes' was held and put into practice by many worthless lordlings and their hangers-on in the novels. But the better-known form of that opinion, namely that drink is the ruin of the working class, was disastrously justified by the gin-soaking in Victorian London. Dickens does not spare us details of the debauchery with drinking caused by the vile conditions in which so many were living.

Boz in his twenty-third *Sketch* discussing gin-shops emphasises the fact that they flourished in a most glittering and alluring form with plenty of plate glass, immense lamps, and illuminated clocks at the corner of every street where the slums were darkest and dirtiest. 'The gin-shops in and near Drury Lane, Holborn, St Giles's, Covent Garden and Clare Market are the handsomest in London. There is more of filth and squalid misery near those great thoroughfares than in any part of this mighty city.' He then described the teeming, ill-drained, decaying tenements or 'rookeries', which he was later to present again in Tom-All-Alone's, and stressed the contrast offered by the warmth and blazing lights of the bars, where the customers with a copper to spare were invited to sample bottles labelled 'The Real Knock-me-Down', 'The Out and Out', 'The Regular Flare-up' and so on. As the night wore on the flare-up began and the police came in to remove to the station-house those who had passed from a sodden escape from misery to the violence of a knock-me-down temper. The *Sketch* ends with a warning to the Temperance Societies that the causes of alcoholism were 'the hunger, filth, and foul air' combined with the cheapness of the liquor. Oblivion was to be bought for 'a pittance which divided among the family would furnish a morsel of bread for each'. But the drunkard took more kicks than ha'pence home to his wife and children in the reeking slum hard by.

To us who rely so much upon the refrigerator the old insistence on warm drinks is surprising. The drinking of port at and after dinner was a diminishing habit in Dickens's time, but mulled port was liked on a cold night and brandy was usually ordered with hot water or as Sam Weller's 'luke'. Whisky was still restricted to the nations who distilled it. It was the heavy malt whisky, which is excellent, especially with a little peat-flavoured water from a hillside burn, for those who are spending a long day of work or sport in the open; but it is not so agreeable to people in towns or sedentary workers. When the blended and lighter whiskies came in at the end of the nineteenth century they were much liked, especially when taken with an aerated water. They soon ousted brandy as the casual or night-time drink of richer folk. But that was after Dickens's time. For the man in the tavern, as well as the man about town, it was brandy and still more brandy, well warmed.

For the less elegant it was beer and gin, mixed in a Dog's Nose, Purl or Flip, or taken separately. Mrs Gamp, when going out as a night-nurse, gave her orders thus for her nourishment and comfort during the hours of her expected vigilance:

> 'I think, young woman,' said Mrs Gamp to the assistant chambermaid, in a tone expressive of weakness, 'that I could pick a little bit of pickled salmon, with a nice little sprig of fennel, and a sprinkling of white pepper. I takes new bread, my dear, with jest a little pat of fresh butter, and a mossel of cheese. In case there should be such a thing as a cowcumber in the 'ouse, will you be so kind as bring it, for I'm

rather partial to 'em, and they does a world of good in a sick-room. If they draws the Brighton Tipper here, I takes *that* ale at night, my love, it being considered wakeful by the doctors. And whatever you do, young woman, don't bring more than a shilling's-worth of gin-and-water warm when I rings the bell a second time, for that is always my allowance, and I never takes a drop beyond!'

Now in winter hot punch is occasionally mixed for a party and the company probably pretends to more enjoyment than it actually gets. We like our gin with tonic water as cold as may be. Ours is indeed the Ice Age in refreshment, whether it be the frozen bar or lolly of the child or the product of a cocktail cabinet for the seniors. The mixing of gin with hot water sounds almost nauseous to modern taste, and in few, if any, public-houses is a kettle ready boiling in or behind the bar for supplying the hot drinks which the Victorians thought essential to inner comfort. Those with empty stomachs got their refocillation that way. And those already well lined with victuals or about so to line themselves were equally determined to begin and end their stoking up with recourse to a glass of wine mulled in a manner named after a certain connoisseur of warmth called Colonel Negus or with a bowl of punch in which the spirits and other ingredients were almost on the boil. The 'social glass' for the Dickensians was a steaming one.

CHAPTER NINE

Going to School

DICKENS died in the year in which a national system of education was born. The Act which William Forster, a Bradford manufacturer by profession and a Quaker by religion, steered through Parliament in 1870 made education free and compulsory. Henceforward there would be schools for all, if they did not dodge them, and there would be an official to catch the artful dodgers and cope with the selfish parents who would rather have their children earning a shilling or two on the streets than learning to read a book or two in a classroom. As G. M. Young put it in his survey of Victorian England called *Portrait of an Age*, 'The Beadle, a vanishing figure of fun, underwent a strange rejuvenation into the School Board Man, the Attendance Officer, and how forcible and disturbing his appearance was we may divine from the consideration that in Birmingham before the Act forty children out of a hundred, in Manchester fifty, were running loose in the streets.'

The new arrangements were controlled by School Boards, whose members were appointed by local elections. Dickens often fulminated against boards and he might have not liked those set up to look after the new schools. But he could hardly have failed to approve of Mr Forster's Act, which put the responsibility for combating illiteracy, an evil not even yet wholly defeated, on the taxpayers and ratepayers and their chosen representatives. The start was slow, the progress was slow, but a disgrace to the nation had been partially ended.

What had been going on before that? For the poorer classes there was an anarchy of religious sectarian schooling with the sects intolerant of each other and shamefully contentious, and a scanty supply of amateurish school-teaching in home premises for the tiny fees which were all that the pupils could bring, or else there was nothing at all. A specimen of the amateur dame-school, no doubt caricatured, is to be seen in the teaching administered to young Pip by Mr Wopsle's great-aunt in *Great Expectations* (chapter 7). This lady conducted her educational operations for an hour or so after closing her little village shop.

> She was a ridiculous old woman of limited means and unlimited infirmity, who used to go to sleep from six to seven every evening, in the society of youth who paid twopence per week each, for the improving opportunity of seeing her do it. She rented a small cottage, and Mr Wopsle had the room upstairs, where we students used to overhear him reading aloud in a most dignified and terrific manner, and occasionally bumping on the ceiling. There was a fiction that Mr Wopsle 'examined' the scholars, once a quarter. What he did on those occasions was to turn up his cuffs, stick up his hair, and give us Mark Antony's oration over the body of Caesar.

But the children, if sufficiently alert, did somehow learn to read and count despite the inertia of the great-aunt, whose activities were limited to an occasional scurry with a birch-rod. Pip recounts of this schooling:

> I struggled through the alphabet as if it had been a bramble-bush; getting considerably worried and scratched by every letter. After that, I fell among those thieves, the nine figures, who seemed every evening to do something new to disguise themselves and baffle recognition. But, at last I began, in a purblind groping way, to read, write, and cipher, on the very smallest scale.

The novels have several similar establishments, not all of them as ludicrous as this one.

To couple schooling with the name of Dickens is immediately to suggest Dotheboys Hall since *Nicholas Nickleby* is one of his books most widely read. The picture of Mr Squeers and his fantastically barbaric establishment certainly had a foundation of fact. After he had finished *Oliver Twist* in 1838, Dickens, both to expose a scandal and to find material for the story of *Nicholas Nickleby*, made a winter journey by coach to north Yorkshire in the company of his illustrator, Hablot Browne, who signed his work as 'Phiz'. There had been much talk in the south of a cruel pretence of education carried on in lonely northern districts by unscrupulous rogues who put out spacious advertisements of excellent instruction in ancient and modern languages, mathematics, and other curriculum features and guaranteed 'no vacations'. This meant that they offered a dumping-ground for the unwanted children of pitiless parents or for orphans whose guardians would pay twenty guineas a year to be completely rid of their responsibility and not see the victims again for a very long time. With no holidays the children could not get home to describe their treatment and their letters could be censored and controlled. The master could be an ignorant ruffian since with no state system of education there could be no system of compulsory inspection, and there were profits to be made by exploiting the wretched little creatures committed to these places.

The tip of Yorkshire which borders on Durham was reputed to be a nest of such schools, and Dickens, having driven two hundred and forty miles up the Great North Road in weather perhaps as severe as that endured by his Nickleby, stayed at Barnard Castle on the Tees and sought information from the locals including a clock-maker called Master Humphrey, whose name reappears in the story so entitled. He learned that a village called Bowes was notorious for several of these schools and especially for one kept by a Mr Shaw, to whom he obtained a letter of introduction.

Bowes is four miles west of Barnard Castle on the old Roman road which leads over some high bleak moors to Penrith, Carlisle, and the far corner of the Roman Wall. It is a thousand feet up and when it is cold there it is cold indeed. Recently the Roman road has become a roaring thoroughfare of cars and lorries speeding to and from Scotland. But those who stop there will find a village in which English history is strikingly epitomised since it contains the remnants of a Roman bath used by the legionaries plodding to and from the Wall, has many Roman relics in the church, a Norman castle, and the house which, when I first knew it, was called Alderson's Farm and is now labelled, no doubt correctly, Dotheboys Hall. It is quite small and if Mr Shaw huddled forty boys into it they were tightly packed. How much Dickens really saw of the school's working is uncertain. Shaw, whom he was to present to the world as Mr Squeers, while he was careful not to mention Bowes or Shaw by name, would hardly welcome visitors if the boys were the prisoners of such a Belsen as Dickens was to describe.

There were certainly cases of outrageous neglect in the Yorkshire schools and the Bowes churchyard is said to contain many graves of the boys who died there. I cannot verify this because the names and dates on old gravestones become obscure. But that Shaw was such a monster as the avaricious, sadistic, and conscienceless swindler and torturer Squeers is rather hard to believe. Visitors to Dickens House in Doughty Street in London will be surprised by the exhibits from Bowes, which show that some at least of the pupils could write a good hand and were well advanced in arithmetic. We need not put too much trust in the letter sent home by Master Dobson saying that he is 'well in health and very happy' since that could have been dictated with Mr Shaw, cane in hand, behind him. But the standard of literacy and mathematics is far above that suggested in the account of Dotheboys.

There were deaths (the Victorians took a certain amount of

infantile and juvenile mortality for granted), but we can discover that Shaw paid three pounds, five shillings, and elevenpence for a pupil's gravestone. Since the fees mentioned by Dickens are twenty guineas for fifty-two weeks of keep and supposed tuition this is an expenditure which could have set the Dickensian Squeers swooning with shock. The sum may have been recoverable from a parent or guardian, and one of that kind heartless enough to send a boy to a Yorkshire school may have thought the cost of a grave to be reasonably earned by the removal of a young nuisance. Heartless they must have been since it is hard to believe, with all the rumours of gross ill-treatment in the air, that any humane person would have boarded a child in such a place without some previous investigation.

But that Shaw was as utterly devilish as Squeers is painted is unlikely for another reason. Bowes is an isolated moorland village of a thousand inhabitants and certainly was no larger and probably rather smaller at the time of Dickens's visit. In so small a community all would know what was going on at the school in their midst. Yorkshire people are warm-hearted as well as tough-sinewed. Dickens introduces a local farmer of this kindly nature in Mr Browdie and such folk would not have endured in their midst the existence of a torture-chamber run by a merciless robber like Squeers. This is not to say that Shaw and his kind were not rightly exposed. But we must allow for some exaggeration in the picture of the non-stop flogging of the ragged, half-frozen, and starving waifs at Dotheboys. The scandal was there, however, and the exposure of it by a novelist who had already won many thousands of readers greatly assisted its termination.

Because *David Copperfield* was partly autobiographical there has been a tendency to suppose that Mr Creakle's appalling academy called Salem House is a picture of a school which Dickens attended. But it is a great mistake to assume that *David Copperfield* contains close portraiture. Darling Dora is linked with the Maria Beadnell who roused a juvenile and for a time deeply felt infatuation in the young lawyer's clerk that Dickens then was, but Maria can hardly have been quite such a complete booby and helpless innocent as David's girl-wife was to become in the story. Nor is it likely that Miss Beadnell, who had rejected rather scornfully the impassioned youngster, could have become as wander-witted and richly absurd as Flora Finching, who is supposed to be a portrait of Maria as seen by the author in a later state of disillusion.

Dickens's father, John Dickens, was sadly improvident and no doubt as amusingly optimistic as Mr Micawber, with whom he is identified; but it is worth noting that John Dickens could hold his job as a naval pay clerk and return to it after imprisonment for debt, and that he was later awarded a 'retired allowance' of one hundred and forty-five pounds a year after twenty years' service, which was no trivial amount then and indicates approval of his work. With this in hand John next got work with his brother-in-law, J. H. Barrow, editor of *The Mirror of Parliament*, as a political reporter. Mr Barrow's kindness to a kinsman doubtless helped in that, but the retired Civil Servant did successfully learn shorthand and practised it well enough, a feat most unlikely in the fictional Micawber, although he did show some power of manoeuvre in the overthrow of Uriah Heep and later (and almost incredibly) became an esteemed magistrate in Australia. *David Copperfield* is a novel and its characters are, in part, glorious fictions.

There is therefore reason to take Mr Creakle as almost a caricature. Salem House is a boarding-school and Dickens was never a boarder, either with Mr Giles at Rochester in his childhood or later at the 'Classical and Commercial Academy' called Wellington House conducted by Mr Jones in the Hampstead Road. Here he was a pupil from 1824 to 1826 and possibly for some months in 1827. The Salem House presented in *David Copperfield* is not far removed in squalor and brutality from Dotheboys and Creakle may be called a minor version of the ogre that was Squeers. Coarse and ignorant, he regarded teaching and thrashing as identical, mixing a very small ration of the former with a very large one of the latter. David wrote of him:

> I should think there never can have been a man who enjoyed his profession more than Mr Creakle did. He had a delight in cutting at the boys, which was like the satisfaction of a craving appetite. I am confident that he couldn't resist a chubby boy especially; that there was a fascination in such a subject, which made him restless in his mind until he had scored and marked him for the day. I was chubby myself, and ought to know. I am sure, when I think of the fellow now, my blood rises against him with the disinterested indignation I should feel if I could have known all about him without having ever been in his power; but it rises hotly, because I know him to have been an incapable brute, who had no more right to be possessed of the great trust he held than to be Lord High Admiral, or Commander-in-chief—in either of which capacities it is probable that he would have done infinitely less mischief.

There may have been a closer model in one of Mr Jones's ushers, the pitiful Mr Mell with the shame of his mother's pauperism, his inability to keep order, his boots beyond repair, and the fearful sense of frustration which made him 'talk to himself sometimes and grin and clench his fist and grind his teeth and pull his hair in an unaccountable manner'. Mr Mell, with his only consolation a flute, is real in a way which the odious Creakle is not. The squalid, ink-splashed, smelly school-room could be an exaggerated version of the premises at Wellington House. But if people were suggesting that Dickens was hitting at this establishment in particular and not at bad schools in general in his portrait of Salem House, he took care to put them right. This he did in an article which he wrote in 1851 for *Household Words*, the magazine which he was editing, and published later in his *Reprinted Pieces*.

The subject of the article called 'Our School' is obviously Wellington House, since it is exactly localised by the statement at the beginning that the railway had sliced away a part of it. The London to Birmingham line from the adjacent Euston Station had done that when it burrowed under the Hampstead Road. The glimpse of the premises offered by the revisiting old boy is not encouraging. The pet birds and mice kept by boys in the school-room are there as in Salem House. The headmaster is no man of learning and is fond of smiting the palms with a ruler and the pantaloons with a cane. But he is scarcely a Creakle and his establishment, 'a school of some celebrity in its neighbourhood', has a fair-sized staff.

Dickens, on entering at the age of twelve, was at once 'put into Virgil' and had the honour to obtain and hold the eminent position of first boy. There was an usher who taught a number of subjects and was liked by all. He had a good knowledge of boys and would have made it a much better school if he had had more power. There is a shadow of Mell, the Salem usher, in this gentle-faced fellow who was crossed in love and was given to relieving his feelings with a broken trombone as the wretched Mell did with his flute.

The Latin master was 'colourless, doubled-up, near-sighted and lame' but 'a very good scholar who took great pains where he saw intelligence and a desire to learn', qualities plainly to be found in the boy Dickens. The school had also 'a fat little dancing master who taught the horn-pipes' and 'a brisk little French master'. So there were chances for an energetic and precocious boy to get ahead, and taken they were by him who after twenty-five years was to write with a certain sympathy but no great admiration about 'Our School'.

We can take Wellington House to be an average specimen of the fee-paying school to which the middle-class London fathers with small or moderate incomes were sending their sons. It had a few parlour-boarders but was mostly a day-school. The more prosperous and rapidly expanding professional and business families during Dickens's lifetime were seeking better education for their children and their demand was met by the foundation of new public schools, as they were and still are called; the title is absurd and misleading since they are essentially private. The historic schools of this kind, such as Eton, Harrow, Westminster, Shrewsbury, Winchester, and Rugby, could no longer contain the number of would-be entrants and to them were added a succession of similar establishments most of whose pupils were boarders. These early Victorian foundations included Marlborough, Cheltenham, Radley, and Lancing in the eighteen-forties; Wellington and Clifton came in the next two decades. Some had special attachments to the Church of England and two of them, Cheltenham and Wellington, later specialised in preparing candidates for commissions in the Army.

They have been described as 'mimic Etons at popular prices' and they were not free from snobbery and exclusiveness on their own level. Cheltenham for example called itself 'The Gentlemen's College', thus distinguishing itself from the much older local grammar school. A dozen years after its founding in 1840 a parallel boarding-school for girls was started in Cheltenham and this was called 'The Ladies' College'. Scotland followed this model with Fettes College in 1870, breaking both there and elsewhere with the native tradition of day attendance at academies, high schools, and grammar schools.

This world was outside the acquaintance of Dickens in his early years of writing, and if he read *Tom Brown's Schooldays*, written by Thomas Hughes but published anonymously in 1857, he could well decide that Rugby had certain features in common

The Dame's School

A London Board School, late nineteenth century

with Salem House and that its 'muscular Christianity' was more muscular than Christian. Consideration of Dean Farrar's *Eric or Little by Little* (1858) and *St Winifred's* (1862) would hardly persuade him that he had missed much by lacking a college life of the kind there described. Nor were the opinions of his contemporary, Thackeray, about his existence at Charterhouse likely to make him feel that his experiences and instruction at Wellington House were the worst that could have happened to a growing boy. But he did not refrain from sending a son to Eton.

Since he chose usually to write of what he had himself seen and felt, enjoyed, and hated, he said little about universities. He was studying, most fruitfully for his future writing, the peculiarities of the law and lawyers when others of his age were attending (or cutting) lectures at Oxford and Cambridge. He learned about politics by reporting the speeches and watching the performance of politicians instead of by taking a diploma or degree in economics or political science. It was just as well for the sloth, misrule, and bigotry of the universities' administrators and professors at the time that Dickens had never entered one of them. They would have heard all about it later on if he had done so. His readers were thereby deprived of some entertaining reading about the dignitaries of the gown and these dignitaries escaped such a whipping as came to the schoolmasters under the lash of his pen.

Another of the Dickensian schools is in Coketown, where Mr M'Choakumchild is in command. This pedagogue is not presented as an ignorant bully lashing out with tongue and cane like Squeers and Creakle. He has been put through a training-mill and has come out flat, dry, and stuffed with facts, facts, facts, which were so well ground into him that if he ever perspired you feel that only names, dates, and figures seeped through his pores. 'If only he had learned a little less,' was the author's comment, 'how infinitely better he might have taught much more.'

He works in a school which has been instituted by Mr Gradgrind of Coketown for the cramming of the Coketown children with as much factual matter as possible. Mr M'Choakumchild may be in name a master but he is in fact a servant, almost a slave, of Coketown's ruling class, typified by the fact-worshipping Gradgrind and that ruthless employer of the mill-hands, Josiah Bounderby. The latter believes that any of his workers who shows any discontent or asks for a slightly higher wage is demanding to be fed with turtle soup and venison out of a gold spoon. What the school has to produce is youngsters who accept the supposed facts as the economists saw them and have no fanciful notions about a better world. Fancy is 'a word to be discarded altogether'. When Gradgrind is inspecting the school he asks a boy called Bitzer for his definition of a horse; and this answer is received and approved: ' "Quadruped. Graminivorous. Forty teeth, namely twenty-four grinders, four eye-teeth, and twelve incisive. Sheds coat in the spring; in marshy countries, sheds hoofs too. Hoofs hard, but requiring to be shod with iron. Age known by marks in mouth." Thus (and much more) Bitzer.'

It can be said that *Hard Times* is one of Dickens's failures. He had been up to Preston in Lancashire, where a strike was in progress and the Gradgrind-Bounderby type was rampantly dominant. In his disgust Dickens overdid his attack on the dreary steely philosophy of the one and the avaricious tyranny of the other. They are not so much living people as expressions of loathing and contempt. The Coketown school which we are shown may be a justly drawn sardonic picture of a certain kind of dryasdust education. But while we are gripped by the painting of Creakle as an ogre, though knowing him to be overpainted, we may not be persuaded that M'Choakumchild is an actual person; it is significant that Dickens, having introduced him, quickly drops him, bored perhaps by the bore he has created.

Hard Times was driving him half-mad since he was overworked and ill when he wrote it, and he took it away to France to get done with it. There are truly Dickensian passages, especially in the description of the life of the vagrant circus folk, who do not understand economics and do understand animals and human animals too. But the anger with the economists and statisticians which might have fired Dickens to a wonderful blaze of satirical comedy did not work that way. His Coketown is never as convincing as his London or his southern towns and M'Choakumchild's school is much less easily remembered than that of Dr Blimber, to whose care Paul Dombey was committed beside the sea-waves of Brighton which Paul found so evocative. Many who have had a classical education have met Blimberism and suffered.

This Dr Blimber had a grandiose but far from cheerful establishment on the Brighton front. It was 'an educational hot-house in which a forcing apparatus was incessantly at work and where every description of Greek and Latin vegetable was got off the driest twigs of boys under the frostiest circumstances. Nature was of no consequence at all.' The Doctor's pupils came from wealthy homes and were boarded well enough. He was not brutal, merely pompous. The ill-treatment was of the young mind, which was confined in a straitjacket of the ancient world and its languages. The boys were instructed by the Doctor, his daughter, and the usher. Mr Feeder, B.A. 'knew no rest from the pursuit of stony-hearted verbs, savage noun-substantives, inflexible syntactic passages, and ghosts of exercises that appeared to them in their dreams. Under the forcing system, a young gentleman usually took leave of his spirits in three weeks. He had all the cares of the world on his head in three months.'

Miss Blimber was a true child of her father. 'There was no light nonsense about Miss Blimber. She kept her hair short and crisp, and wore spectacles. She was dry and sandy with working in the graves of deceased languages. None of your live languages for Miss Blimber. They must be dead—stone dead—and then Miss Blimber dug them up like a ghoul.'

Mrs Blimber, though not learned, had similar affectations and would announce at evening parties that if she could have known Cicero she thought she would have died contented. Paul Dombey was sickly and doubtless doomed in any case. The forcing process of Blimberism was well calculated to force him rapidly out of this world altogether—and did so.

Dickens, as was recounted, was 'put into Virgil' as soon as he went to Wellington House at the age of twelve, and though the Latin master at 'Our School' was sympathetically described the result of the Virgilian forcing was to leave the pupil with a strong distaste for dead languages. This was perhaps natural in one so vital and so fond of all things fresh and exuberant, alive and kicking.

The more expensive education of the period was shackled in classicism. What was called 'the grand old fortifying curriculum' was very much the essence of Blimberism and continued to be so long after the death of Dickens. It had its merits as a mental discipline. In the hands of an enlivening imaginative master, who could link ancient and modern in a creative way and did not merely follow Miss Blimber's spade-work among the graves of the deceased languages, it could have some quickening power. But such masters were few. The needs of the twentieth century demand some knowledge of science as well as of history which did not finish with the Caesars. Dickens could have found some charitable and encouraging words for many of the schools of today, and he did indeed describe a teacher of whom he could approve most warmly.

That was Dr Strong of Canterbury, to whose well-mannered and well-taught academy David Copperfield was sent by his good aunt, Betsy Trotwood. The Doctor was large, untidy, benevolent, and sympathetic, a scholar devoted to the preparation of a dictionary, which was taking him a very long time. David describes the school thus:

> Doctor Strong's was an excellent school; as different from Mr Creakle's as good is from evil. It was very gravely and decorously ordered, and on a sound system—with an appeal, in everything, to the honour and good faith of the boys, and an avowed intention to rely on their possession of those qualities unless they proved themselves unworthy of it, which worked wonders. We all felt that we had a part in the management of the place, and in sustaining its character and dignity. Hence we soon became warmly attached to it—I am sure I did for one; and I never knew, in all my time, of any other boy being otherwise—and learned with a good will, desiring to do it credit. We had noble games out of hours, and plenty of liberty; but even then, as I remember, we were well spoken of in the town, and rarely did any disgrace, by our appearance or manner, to the reputation of Doctor Strong and Doctor Strong's boys.

Schools of that liberal kind were beginning to flower in the thorny jungle of Victorian education. One was at Bruce Castle, a curious but historically justified name for a building in the district of Tottenham in north London. Here the father of the Scottish hero Robert Bruce had once lived and his mansion, rebuilt in the seventeenth century, has survived to be a museum with a park and playing-field today. Rowland Hill, chiefly famous as a reformer of the postal service, had founded a school there which was recommended by Dickens in 1845 in a letter to the actor Macready for the placing of one of his boys. He wrote that there were difficulties because it was always full. The sons of other authors, Douglas Jerrold and William Howitt, were entered there. Dickens said of this academy that here was the only recognition of education as a broad system of moral and intellectual philosophy of which he knew. 'They have a miscellaneous library,' his letter ran, 'under the management of the boys themselves, of some five or six thousand volumes, and every means of study and recreation and every inducement to self-reliance and self-exertion that can easily be imagined. As there is no room just now you can turn it over in your mind again. And if you would like to see the place yourself, when you return to town, I shall be delighted to go there with you.'

Here is a change indeed from Wellington House and still more from such a ghastly prison as the Christ's Hospital attended and described by Charles Lamb fifty years earlier, an establishment deserving a gaol-name since Lamb recounted that boys endeavouring to run away were put fettered in cells before repeated floggings. But the methods at Bruce Castle were rarely to be found elsewhere and the general quality of scholastic life, whether the parents paid little or much, continued to be based on the assumption that the young were not to be regarded as potentially reliable and having latent qualities to be drawn out, but as limbs of Satan, full of original sin which had either to be sweated out, as Bowen of Harrow believed, by intense application to compulsory games or thrashed out in the manner of the believers in discipline through terror.

Schools for girls do not receive the same attention from Dickens as the ridiculous or sinister academies to which the boys in the novels are sent. The daughters of gentlemen willing to pay liberally are, however, occasionally followed into such hen-coops of refinement as that provided by Miss Monflathers and met by little Nell in *The Old Curosity Shop*. It is the pride of that lady to be trusted with the care of a baronet's daughter while she snubs and bullies the humane Miss Edwards, who is only an impoverished pupil-teacher. The headmistress is a dragon of gentility and determined to keep the other sex completely at bay. Her 'Boarding and Day Establishment' was a large house, with a high wall, and a large garden-gate with a large brass plate, and a small grating through which Miss Monflathers's parlour-maid inspected all visitors before admitting them; for nothing in the shape of a man, no, not even a milk-man, was suffered, without special licence, to pass that gate. Even the tax-gatherer, who was stout, and wore spectacles, and a broad-brimmed hat, had the taxes handed through the grating. More obdurate than gate of adamant or brass, this gate of Miss Monflathers's frowned on all mankind. The very butcher respected it as a gate of mystery, and left off whistling when he rang the bell.

The educational method of Miss Monflathers described as 'applicable to genteel children only' is concentrated mainly on 'painting on velvet, fancy needlework, or embroidery'. That is an escape from dead languages and Blimberism but it is hardly an extensive curriculum. The sheltering of girls from 'good families' and the insistence on decorum as the chief end of schooling was to survive Dickens by many years. When a genuine extension of the curriculum to include a serious attention to the mind as well as to moral correctness and genteel accomplishments of a domestic kind was introduced by the pioneers at Cheltenham and elsewhere their immediate imitators were few.

The well-to-do parents would employ for their daughters a governess, as Dickens did himself, or possibly an instructress who disdained that title. Such was the formidable Mrs General invited by Mr Dorrit, when restored to affluence, to complete the education, such as it had been, of his daughters Fanny and Amy. The child of a highly placed ecclesiastic, the widow of an army martinet, carrying a sheaf of bogus laudatory testimonials, Mrs General is described as 'cool, waxy, and blown-out'. 'Putting ideas into young heads' was her idea of vicious practice. Heads were not made for ideas. Her purpose was to have no opinions and to discourage opinions in her pupils. Like Mr Podsnap she waved aside all views found distasteful. 'This was another of her ways of forming a mind—to cram all articles of difficulty into cupboards, lock them up, and say that they had no existence. It was the easiest way and, beyond all comparison, the properest. . . . The little that was left in the world, when all these deductions were made, it was Mrs General's province to varnish.' And as a polisher of nothingness her educational technique was most impressive. One feels that if she had got hold of Miss Monflathers she could have varnished even her.

Her views on speech, however, had some positive quality. She achieved perpetual remembrance by this advice on the correct way to speak to a parent:

> 'Papa' is a preferable form of address. . . . 'Father' is rather vulgar, my dear. The word papa, besides, gives a pretty form to the lips. Papa, potatoes, poultry, prunes, and prism, are all very good words for the lips—especially prunes and prism. You will find it serviceable, in the formation of a demeanour, if you sometimes say to yourself in company—on entering a room, for instance—papa, potatoes, poultry, prunes and prism, prunes and prism.

Mrs General is unforgettable, just as one of the Dickensian schoolmasters, Charlie Hexam in *Our Mutual Friend*, is intolerable. He is prig and snob, a most unworthy brother of his faultless sister Lizzie. Another pedagogue in that book is Bradley Headstone, who behaves like a madman in the grip of his love for that humble heroine. Poor Mr Mell and dear Dr Strong are lonely exceptions to Dickens's general dislike of teachers and their teaching. But we must remember that he lived at a time when schooling was scanty or absent among the poor, and narrow and hide-bound among the rich.

Better things were coming. Oxford and Cambridge Universities began to shake off their lethargy and the bigotry of their religious tests for academic posts. The fellows of the colleges were released from their obligation to be unmarried and this brought in a new range of talents to teaching. Benjamin Jowett became Master of Balliol in the year of Dickens's death and was able to institute as well as advocate long-needed reforms. Quite early in the lifetime of Dickens, London University had been founded to take in the Nonconformists and secularists, who were excluded from Oxford and Cambridge. At London the curriculum was much wider and modern studies including the sciences were developed. One may wonder how Dickens would have liked it and gained by it if he had gone there after leaving Wellington House. He may have learned more of human nature, which was to be the raw material of his life-work, in lawyers' offices. The schools too were at last ceasing to be the wretched and poorly staffed places of which he wrote, and his writing had indirectly been a considerable incentive to their gradual increase in humanity and competence.

CHAPTER TEN

Faith and Works

DURING the lifetime of Dickens the religious life of England was steadily but slowly reformed, and reform was desperately needed. There were many evils to be eradicated. Intolerance had to be overcome. In 1829 the Catholic Emancipation Act admitted Roman Catholics to Parliament and to most of the civil and military posts in the service of the state, from which they had previously been barred by their faith. But Protestantism remained dominant and suspicious. In 1850 the Pope resolved to establish dioceses of the Roman Church in this country and this was widely and bitterly resented as 'papal aggression'. But the ever increasing flow of Irish immigrants added largely to the numbers of working-class Catholics in England, while the influence of the Anglican Newman, who renounced the living of St Mary's in Oxford in 1843, was received into the Roman Church in 1845, was ordained a priest in 1846, and was created a cardinal in 1879, worked powerfully among the intellectuals.

Elsewhere too, Anglo-Catholicism was growing strong; it had the aesthetic appeal of decorative ritual, which the Evangelical Protestants detested, it was more liberal in its view of a Christian Sunday, and it was much readier to associate the gospel of Christianity with social reform. Yet the intolerance of Oxford and Cambridge towards Dissenters, unbelievers, and heretics of any kind was only slowly broken down. The Universities Act of 1854 had in theory opened Oxford and Cambridge to Nonconformists, but until 1871, when all religious tests were removed, the various colleges could make what conditions they chose, and some were stubbornly and exclusively Anglican in their policy of admission. C. P. Scott, who was later to be the renowned editor of the *Manchester Guardian*, went to Oxford in 1865, but he was rejected by two colleges of his choice because he came of a Unitarian family. He was accepted at Corpus Christi College, where there were more open minds in authority.

Though there was a new and quickening spirit in the Church of England, and there was even a beginning of Christian Socialism, many Anglican clergy had by no means shaken off the sloth and corruption which had been so conspicuous in the previous century. A remarkable scandal was exposed at Rochester in the heart of the Dickens country. The story of some astonishing behaviour by the Dean and Chapter of Rochester Cathedral fortunately received considerable publicity, and the affair was described in detail by Mr Ralph Arnold in a book called *The Whiston Matter*, published in 1961.

Whiston was a vigorous young clergyman-schoolmaster with a distinguished academic career who was appointed to the headship of the Rochester Cathedral Grammar School in 1842. The school had faded to nothing because the previous headmaster was said to have flogged all the boys away. When Whiston set about filling a school which was completely empty he discovered that the terms of the foundation, which dated back to the time of Henry VIII, had been shockingly broken. Under their statutes the Dean and Chapter were to give free maintenance to each Grammar School boy and pay him a stipend of two pounds thirteen shillings and fourpence a year for his expenses. They were also entrusted to maintain four poor scholars at Oxford and Cambridge with a stipend of five pounds a year for four years and a little more if they stayed on after taking their degrees. That sum was deemed sufficient for a student in the sixteenth century, but in the eighteen-forties the money for maintenance at a university should certainly have been increased by at least twelve times. The Dean and Chapter had let the Grammar School collapse and had also neglected the university obligation, while their own salaries had been largely increased. Whiston accused them roundly of neglecting the trust and lining their own pockets. He was dismissed from his post and only reinstated after a long battle in which he drove home a powerful case against many more cathedral clerics than those at Rochester.

In a pamphlet issued in 1849 called *Cathedral Trusts and their Fulfilment* Whiston revealed an appalling state of affairs. At Canterbury the statutes allotted a stipend of four pounds a year to each Cathedral Grammar School boy, but the boys were getting only a third of that and none of the free maintenance which was their due. The balance was illegally taken by the clerics who were their masters. The researches made by Whiston discovered similar robbery of the pupils at Worcester, Ely, and Chester, and revealed the fact that the Bishop of Rochester was also acting as Dean of Worcester and drawing from Worcester a stipend of nearly fifteen hundred pounds a year, while the Grammar Boys there were getting only five shillings and tenpence a year instead of their statutory two pounds thirteen shillings and fourpence.

The Whiston case gave Trollope some useful material for his book *The Warden* and for his other stories of life at his imagined, but realistic, cathedral town of Barchester. The exposure of ecclesiastical theft did not in the end deprive the indomitable Whiston of his modest position as headmaster of a small Cathedral Grammar School. But it did deny him promotion in the Church, where he had certainly more right to be a bishop than many of those then in charge of a diocese. Fortunately his courageous defiance of deans and canons, who were filling their own pockets by cheating the students while deriving comfortable and growing stipends from the cathedral funds, was made widely known. The

Church of England, thus put in the pillory, had to purge its guilt by drastic reforms.

The Church could be fairly represented as a black-coated branch of the social and political establishment and infected with its vices. If Coodle, Doodle, and Foodle ruled at Westminster their relatives might expect a share of the episcopal palaces, comfortable deaneries, and free quarters in the pleasant houses of the canons in cathedral precincts. If the higher clergy were not Coodles or members of the Tite Barnacle family they behaved no better, as the Whiston case plainly showed, and they were disgracefully neglecting and misusing their educational responsibilities. Yet Dickens, to whom the socially powerful cliques were hateful, appears less hostile to the Anglican Church than to the chapels, whose gaseous and self-righteous pastors and preachers he satirised repeatedly and with virulence. In the Rochester of *Edwin Drood* he put the excellent Mr Crisparkle and in *Our Mutual Friend* there appear Mr and Mrs Milvey, most likeable examples of the hard-working cleric and his wife in a poor parish.

During the eighteenth century the sluggishness and complacency of the Church of England had been vigorously and effectively challenged by John and Charles Wesley, and the ranks of the Dissenters then contained many devoted men as well as excellent preachers. But Nonconformity, as Dickens saw it, had lost its inspiration and declined into a repulsive mixture of narrow, even hypocritical, piety and empty rhetoric. In his articles called 'Sunday Under Three Heads' he described with contempt religion abused by both sections of the Faith. First there was the fashionable Anglican Church in which 'the powdered footmen glide along the aisle, place the richly-bound prayer-books on the pew desks, slam the doors and hurry away, leaving the fashionable members of the congregation to inspect each other through their glasses and to dazzle and glitter in the eyes of the few shabby people in the free seats'. The clergyman who takes the service has been celebrated at Eton for his stupidity and at Cambridge for his knowledge of horses and dancers. The 'sleek Divine' who preaches does so briefly 'in a voice kept down by rich feeding' and murmurs only 'comfortable doctrines'.

A sad picture, but not as angry as the one which follows. In the chapel of 'the less orthodox' there is a coarse hard-faced minister who puts up a tremendous act, gesturing, perspiring, threatening damnation, and making the women moan and sway and even faint as 'he blasphemously calls upon the Deity to visit with eternal torments those who turn aside from the Word—as interpreted and preached by himself'. Dickens had good reason to respect the finer aspects of Nonconformity since he was himself no conformer to the Victorian standards of right and wrong. But as a humane man he was revolted by the inhumanity of the dealers in hell-fire.

This religion of wrath could be found in the church as well as in the chapel. David Copperfield remembered Miss Murdstone with her 'austere and wrathful' religion 'emphasising all the dread words with a cruel relish'. When Mr Chillip says 'I don't find authority for Mr and Mrs Murdstone in the New Testament' David heartily agrees. Dickens was a New Testament Christian, and much of his hatred of the Dissenting preachers of his time was caused by their insistence on the anger of the Old Testament's Jehovah instead of on the compassion of Jesus in the New. He mocked these pulpit-bangers with semi-biblical names such as Melchizedek Howler, and he loathed their assumption of a shepherd's good qualities while they disciplined their flock with menaces of eternal punishment.

Very early in his writing he had lashed out at Shepherd Stiggins in *The Pickwick Papers* and also at the preacher of perdition in the Little Bethel frequented in pious timidity by Mrs Nubbles in *The Old Curiosity Shop*. Later, in *Bleak House*, there was to be the oily, gluttonous, and word-spinning Chadband, who put his 'fluence' on Mrs Snagsby, but not on her husband, while he laid into their high teas. Chadband may have been church or chapel, since he is described as of 'no particular denomination'. 'What is Terewth?' drawled that greasy orator and answered it by 'climbing a whole series of verbal stairs, arriving by way of his rhetorical questions on a top floor of meaningless platitude'.

It has been complained that Dickens was unfair to all who had 'Reverend' in front of their names. But two examples of admiration for good work well done have been cited, and at the close of his 'Sunday Under Three Heads' he recounted his visit to a country church in the west of England, its churchyard as sweet as a country meadow. 'The impressive service of the Church of England was spoken, not merely read, by a grey-headed minister

'In the meadow beyond the churchyard a very animated game of cricket'
—*Sunday Under Three Heads*

and the responses were delivered by his auditors with an air of sincere devotion as far removed from affectation and display as from coldness and indifference.' The clergyman preached simply and sensibly and after the service was on easy jocular terms with his friendly parishioners. On Sunday evening he not only watched but encouraged a game of cricket, of which game he had once been a great player. Games on Sunday would have put Chadband off his food, if that were possible, and caused Melchizedek Howler to scream himself into a paroxysm of pious fury even to the extent of losing that ululating voice. Dickens could bless 'the cloth' when he found good cause for doing so, as he did in this idyllic pastoral scene of sensible piety and innocent uninhibited pleasures.

In the same series of articles on Sunday and the Sabbatarians Dickens vigorously and brilliantly ridiculed a Sunday Observance Bill introduced into the House of Commons in 1836 by Sir Andrew Agnew. To understand the inhumanity of this measure we must remember that the workers of the time had no half-holiday on Saturday and were accustomed on six days of the week to hours of labour which we should think intolerably long. The acceptance of a five-day week would have seemed almost a criminal lunacy to early Victorian employers and a Utopian dream to the employed.

The heads of firms themselves remained at work on Saturday. When Charlotte and Anne Brontë made their surprise call on their publishers, Smith, Elder & Co. in the City, they expected to find a partner to receive them on a Saturday and were not disappointed, as they would be today. Mr Smith was there to welcome them. Attendance at places of work meant, as a rule, six long days for the minor members of the staff and there were no bank holidays to give an occasional breathing-space. Bank holidays were instituted a year after the death of Dickens. Even at Christmas there was respite only for the single day. Bob Cratchit, having had his Christmas, had no hope of spending a Boxing Day with his family.

It is true that he was due in at nine on that morning and actually arrived eighteen and a half minutes late, but 'he was on his stool in a jiffy, driving away with his pen, as if he were trying to overtake nine o'clock.' Fortunately he was met by a converted Scrooge.

During the boyhood and youth of Dickens, as has been explained, there were no limits to the working-hours, even of children, in the mills and factories. Consequently the freedom to enjoy Sunday in the open was of sovereign importance to the health and happiness of the people. There was little enough of that liberty without the further bondage which Sir Andrew Agnew sought to impose. Many of the workers, as Dickens pointed out, were too tired by their six long days and too poor to make regular excursions into the country; also they had no likelihood of games or sports available if they escaped from the slums and the mean streets to the edge of the town. But the churches and chapels were open, and so, in strange contrast, were the taverns and the gin-palaces. Picturing the jaded and impecunious worker at the end of his sixty-hour week (and it was often a longer week before the Act of 1847), Dickens denounced the Sabbatarians, who made liquor the only alternative to loafing.

> . . . you hold out no inducement, you offer no relief from listlessness, you provide nothing to amuse his mind, you afford him no means of exercising his body. Unwashed and unshaven, he saunters moodily about, weary and dejected. In lieu of the wholesome stimulus he might derive from nature, you drive him . . . to the gin-shop as his only resource; and when, reduced to a worse level than the lowest brute in the scale of creation, he lies wallowing in the kennel, your saintly law-givers lift up their hands to heaven, and exclaim for a law which shall convert the day intended for rest and cheerfulness into one of universal gloom, bigotry, and persecution.

The attack on Agnew's measure was written at the time of its introduction and carried the apt pseudonym of Timothy Sparks. The writer's anger had been sparked off not only by the Bill itself but by the conduct of the Bishop of London in expatiating on 'the vicious addiction of the lower classes to Sunday excursions'. So here the Dickensian wrath was directed quite as much at the Established Church as at the Melchizedek Howlers in the chapels. A particularly odious feature of the Sunday Observance Bill was its unctuous claim to save the workers from 'sacrificing their comforts, health, religious privileges and conscience'. This was to be done by forbidding the employment of any of them in public transport and catering with heavy penalties for breach of these orders. At the same time it exempted from its discipline a whole army of domestic servants, so that the rich might have all the preparation of meals and all the outings in their own carriages that they wanted. As Timothy Sparks observed, 'The Baronet's dinner must be cooked on Sunday, the Bishop's horses must be groomed, and the Peer's carriage must be driven. So the menial servants are put utterly beyond the pale of grace—unless indeed, they are to go to heaven through the sanctity of their masters, and possibly they might think even that rather an uncertain passport.'

The Bill did not in the end become law and Dickens no doubt contributed to that victory. The coaches and cabs were left to ply for fares on Sundays for those who could pay for them, and the popular tea-gardens, threatened with closure by Agnew, were left open for refreshment. But there were no Sunday games or sports and there was still the squalid drunkenness of those who stayed near their wretched homes and made gin their escape from the darkness of a day when all shutters were up but those of the public-house. Even the few with intellectual or artistic tastes were denied the chance to develop them. Galleries and museums were firmly closed on Sundays, and since there was no half-holiday on Saturday and no bank holidays, there could thus be no visits to these places made by such office and factory workers as would have welcomed the chance to do so.

Religion without dogma has been called a body without a skeleton. Dickens would have scorned the idea, replying that religion is not a body but a spirit and has no need of bones. He was no saint and there were faults in his private life, but inhumanity was never one of them. He took the Sermon on the Mount to be the essence of Christianity, and must have found the doctrinal disputation in the Epistles of St Paul tedious and useless, if he ever bothered to plod through them. His faith was impulsive, emotional, and practical.

He did not believe in original sin; the original virtue of the child was implicit in his view of human nature. Sin is a word which occurs scantily in his vocabulary. Crime was what horrified him, an offence against God because it was an offence against man and especially against children. He hated even more than the crimes punishable by law the more common and more dangerous wickedness of physical and mental cruelty, fanatical intolerance, contempt of human rights, and pride in riches and power. Quite simply he wanted people to be happy, enjoying liberty, equality, and fraternity without revolutionary violence as their provider. In so far as the Christianity of his day created this elementary happiness he was its champion. When it took the form of a cramping killjoy austerity or was merely a patter of pious sentiments uttered by hypocrites to cover their own egotistical self-righteousness he was its enraged and eloquent enemy. He was no sectarian or devotee of any one Church since he thought that religion organised was religion corrupted. He could have echoed the saying of Thomas Paine that the world was his country and to do good his religion. Faith without works was a vacuum to Dickens.

He had a masterly hand for describing wickedness either in the average felon or the exceptional fiend, but his attitude to life was that of an innocent and an optimist. As an author he was a giant, but as a thinker he was a child, which does not mean a fool, but a child with a sharp eye for the present wrongs and a gift of hope for the future betterment. As such he came, he saw, he loved, and he hated with the swift unargued reactions of the innocent abroad among the good and bad, which were instinctively recognised as such.

So for him there was to be no time wasted on refinements of theology and no awed respect for the pronouncements of doctrinaire economists or for the supposed wisdom of what is now academically labelled political science. His morals were his politics and his morals came from the heart. It was a Radical agnostic, Lord Morley, who, when told by a young man that all good things come from the heart replied, 'Yes, but they should go round by the head.' Dickens, no agnostic, might have agreed with that, but not, one imagines, with much enthusiasm. His religion was basically cordial, as warm and inspiriting as the cordials which his characters so frequently drink. They took their liquor warm and Dickens did the same with his Christianity. Argumentative theology was iced barley water to him. He would have agreed with Robert Browning that 'God's in his heaven' but would have qualified the following confident assumption that 'all's right with the world'. That all could be right was his belief, but to ensure it meant an unceasing battle with the bullies, the humbugs, and the cruel domination of stale customs and outworn inequitable laws.

He was far from alone in this undenominational unchurchified Christianity. The Radicals and reformers of his time had rarely despaired of or rejected religion. They too had the Sermon on the Mount at the back of their rhetoric on the platform. The Radical politicians, some of whom later moved on to Socialism and were the fathers of the men and women who created the British Labour Party, were simple moralists and not dealers in learned dialectic. They had no interest in the Communism and atheism of Karl Marx, who in the last years of Dickens's life was toiling away in London at the composition of his tremendous book on the nature and expected decay of capitalism. The first volume of that closely argued and not easily readable work appeared in 1873, and during the ensuing century it was to shake the world and determine the lives of hundreds of millions of people in Europe and Asia, most of whom incidentally have never read the book and have only been converted to Marxism by fanatical Marxians with a ruthless use of force to back their promises of an earthly paradise.

Most of the leaders of the British working class during the nineteenth century were hardly influenced at all by Continental Socialism and Communism. They had been brought up on the Bible and they based their politics on the ethics of Christianity as they saw it. Some of the reformers stated openly that they aimed at being agents of the Divine Will, an idea which would have been scorned by Karl Marx. Humphrey House in his book on *The Dickens World* quoted a pamphlet issued in 1817 whose full title ran:

> The Voice of God!!! In support of the Grand Object of Parliamentary Reform. O ye Noblemen, Clergymen, Gentlemen, Tradesmen, Working Men, and Poor Men, of Great Britain and Ireland, Hear ye the Word of the Lord.
>
> 'By their fruits ye shall know them.'
> Christ.

The author then drew on the prophet Nehemiah, who wrote of the people burdened with mortgaging their lands, vineyards, and houses to the usurers: 'Then I consulted with myself, and I rebuked the nobles, and the rulers, and said unto them, "Ye exact usury, every one of his brother." And I set a great assembly against them.' (Nehemiah 5:7)

A great assembly defending the poor. That was the ideal of those campaigning for an extension of the franchise and an end to the scandal of the pocket boroughs, whose representation in the House of Commons was the gift of the great landlords, themselves mostly members of the House of Lords. There were abundant reasons for creating a Parliament with at least some claim to be democratic without reference to the Old Testament, but to some of the agitators it was necessary to claim Jehovah as their champion.

The Radicals of Dickens's time were readers, and not only of the Bible. The appeals of Robert Burns for human brotherhood and the destruction of privilege were often in their minds and warming their hearts. It is true that the politics of Burns were, like the Scots' haggis, 'fine confused feeding'. He had a sentimental affection for the house of Stuart, on which Dickens in his *Child's History of England* poured ridicule and detestation. It is unlikely that if Bonnie Prince Charlie had won the throne back for his family there would have been any royal recognition that 'the rank is but the guinea-stamp'. Burns, who welcomed the French Revolution, seems never to have been quite clear whether he was a Jacobin or a Jacobite. But he had the genius for putting a simple and generous emotion in the simplest of words which strike to the heart and linger on the lips. So while some of the democrats were quoting the Bible others were echoing

> It's coming yet, for a' that,
> That man to man the warld o'er
> Shall brothers be for a' that.

Dickens, like Burns, was widely read by working men and his denunciations of misrule were made the text for political preaching on the Radical platforms.

In some of the pulpits too there was a growing evidence of Christian shame at the contrast of bitter poverty with abounding wealth. In the Church of England there was a stirring of what may be called Christian Socialism and a revolt against the sluggish acceptance of the state of the nation, or rather, as the progressive

'Our pew in Church' by Phiz

Conservative Disraeli put it, the state of the two nations, one small and rich, the other large and poor. This was manifest among the more intelligent Dissenters, whose existence Dickens strangely and unfairly overlooked. He was so disgusted by the cant and humbug and threats of hell-fire in the minor bethels and Ebenezer chapels that he concentrated on the fanatics and frauds like Stiggins and the gloomy rhetoricians. But the Unitarians, who preached the brotherhood of man under the leadership of Jesus in the service of the one God, and were described by Bernard Shaw as making scepticism respectable, attracted the sympathy of Dickens. They contained in their congregations and counted among their ministers many men of intellectual distinction and advanced views. Remarkable among these was Joseph Priestley, a prominent scientist as well as a Dissenting minister and democratic orator. At the time of the French Revolution he was driven out of the country when the reactionary mob in Birmingham burned his books and scientific equipment and endangered his life. The Priestley tradition of advanced thinking was maintained in Unitarian circles, most notably by Stopford Brooke (1832–1916), who had been a Royal Chaplain in the Anglican Church but went over to Unitarianism in 1880. There were 'men of light and leading' in the chapels as well as canting vessels of wrath and darkness.

The guiding spirits in the Church of England movement towards Christian Socialism were Charles Kingsley (1819–75) and Frederick Denison Maurice (1805–72). Kingsley, who remained a country vicar at Eversley, Hampshire, despite offers of preferment, is most remembered for his story-telling in *Water Babies* and *Westward Ho!* and for some poems which became very popular. But in the novel *Alton Locke*, published in 1850, he had entered the Dickens territory of social portraiture and the disclosure of abuses. His Socialism did not go far and was abandoned when he suspected that it might lead to violence. Maurice was a professor of English literature as well as a cleric with political opinions far in advance of those then held by most prelates and parsons in the Church of England. He was particularly active in promoting adult education and in 1854 was one of the founders of 'The Working Men's College' in

Camden Town, close to where Dickens spent some of his boyhood and went to his school in the Hampstead Road.

The tentative advance of the Christian Socialists was subsequently carried on more vigorously by George Lansbury, an East Ender born in 1859 who led the Labour Party in the House of Commons from 1931 to 1935. Unlike most of his colleagues who had been brought up in one or other of the Nonconformist sects Lansbury remained an Anglican and a regular worshipper. He was a much tougher fighter for democratic policies, including female suffrage, than the early parson-Socialists had been and he was ready to go to prison for a cause. But such men did owe something to the pioneering in ecclesiastical society done by Kingsley and Maurice when that society was mostly Conservative in the extreme and believed that

> The rich man in his castle,
> The poor man at his gate,

were not thus separated by the rich man's superior power and readiness to exploit it. This state of affairs was ordained by Providence:

> God made them, high or lowly,
> And order'd their estate.

The hymn in which those well-known lines occurred was written by the wife of the Archbishop of Armagh in Northern Ireland, who if he approved the opinion of a class society divinely commanded, as he probably did, was certainly not alone among the higher and lower clergy in accepting that complacent creed so convenient for dwellers in the episcopal palaces as well as in the castles of the milords.

Dickens was certainly Christian but no Socialist. With his individualist temperament he distrusted institutions of all kinds and the idea of an all-powerful state was a notion of hell on earth to him. Naturally and equally the idea of a religious hierarchy was repellent to his nature. Accordingly the Papacy, with its immensely powerful organisation and its emphasis upon spiritual authority, was one of his enemies. As Humphrey House put it, 'In nothing was Dickens so much of an elementary John Bull as in his hatred of Roman Catholicism. The Pope is the real villain of his *Child's History of England* and *Pictures from Italy* is full of most stagey descriptions of the scenes of inquisitional torture.' He was a humanist and had the satisfaction during his lifetime of seeing the Protestant Churches becoming less detached from public welfare, more aware of the people's material needs, and so more humane, or at least less inhumane. To him the name of Protestantism, if not the forms that it took in church and chapel, was essentially congenial. For his work was an outcry as well as an entertainment and his whole life was a protest.

CHAPTER ELEVEN

The River

DICKENS was a riverside man. In his early boyhood he happily knew the Medway with the orchard scenery on its flanks and the busy coal trade on its surface. At Chatham were the large shipping and naval establishments of the estuary. As a boy in London he walked by the Thames from Southwark to his work at Hungerford Stairs. He had reason to hate that place and its view as well as its name, which was all too apt to the boy's gnawing and unslaked appetite. When he went to offices in the legal quarter the Thames was adjacent for a stroll at midday or after the offices closed. Next, as a Parliamentary reporter, he practised his hard-won but efficient shorthand beside Westminster Bridge, and while enduring dull speeches droned out to the Lords and Commons he may have decided that Wordsworth was right when the spectacle of that region moved him to exclaim, 'Dear God, the very houses seem asleep.' On his return to Kent at Gad's Hill he was beside the estuary again. He was a river-haunted man and his essays and stories are saturated with waters, some shining and some sinister. It is fashionable now to talk of love-hate relationships; the phrase may be applicable here.

The Thames had three faces for Dickens. There is the highway of the pleasure-boats, rowed up to Richmond or steaming with a churn of paddles down to Greenwich, Gravesend, and the Kentish beaches. There is the Port of London with its splendour of substantial sea-going ships coming in or going out on the tide with strange cargoes, smoky with the bustle of the tugs, and jangling with the din of dockyard noises. There is, finally, the eerie and

Sunday out of doors

macabre Thames of foggy nightfalls on the marshes, the river of murders, suicides, and body-snatching and the prowling place of boatmen and wharf-labourers, who were not always so gay as is suggested by the title of Miss Abbey Potterson's snug tavern, The Six Jolly Fellowship Porters.

The Thames of the gay summer outings is met in the *Sketches by Boz*. Part of the merriment lies in the mishaps. Picnic baskets are upset and the oarsmanship is chaotic. All have boasted their powers of navigation and yet all are found to be making a spurious claim to mastery of steering and propelling the chosen vessel. But this makes rather easy fun for a humorist of Dickens's quality. (He could have written *Three Men in a Boat* in the intervals of knocking off a Parliamentary report.) He is better engaged aboard the paddle-steamer which carries the less strenuous down to the Kentish sands and promenades. By 1815 there were steam-packets on the river and before long the prosperous City man would put his family into summer quarters in Kent and travel to and from his work daily by water. There was brisk discussion of the developing potency and utility of steam among the holders of season tickets for this run since it was possible for the travellers to chatter over a dinner on board during the trip home. 'Steam, still in its infancy,' they would say as they applied themselves to their victuals and 'the brandy-and-water cold', which was in great requisition. The liquor flowed; the platitudes flowed too, and the views of the vivacious river and its cool keen air gave general satisfaction to the up-and-down journeyers or the occasional takers of a trip.

For the pleasure-seekers on warm nights the Thames offered the gardens of Vauxhall on the south bank and Cremorne on the north. Vauxhall was much the older and had flourished throughout the eighteenth century, winning the approval of Dr Johnson for its mixture of showmanship, gay exhibitions, and music not too refined for the general ear, all available for a shilling. The glories

Cremorne Gardens 1851, the orchestra

of the more select Ranelagh had ended in 1803; Vauxhall survived till 1859. Oliver Goldsmith said that it united rural beauty with courtly magnificence and concluded that with this at their doors Londoners had no need to go to heaven for paradise. Thackeray in *Vanity Fair* vividly described the myriads of lamps and ravishing melodies (with dark walks for the lovers), the rich feasting in their private boxes, and the contented drinking of pots of stout by those less wealthy.

Boz went to see Vauxhall before nightfall and thought it a great mistake to expose the nocturnal make-believe and magic to the destructive realism of the daylight. 'Our favourite views were mere patches of paint; the fountain that had sparkled so showily by lamp-light presented very much the appearance of a water-pipe that had burst; all the ornaments were dingy and all the walls gloomy.' He should have waited till evening. However, there was the unusual spectacle of a balloon ascent to take the place of fireworks. Vauxhall always had something to astonish and excite.

Another famous garden was opened for festivities in 1843. This was Cremorne, whose Chelsea site is now occupied by Lots Road power station, a substitute more useful, no doubt, but of less amenity. We know of Cremorne through Whistler's paintings and also through a spirited poem called 'The Reminiscences of a Dancing Man' by Thomas Hardy, who was a patron in his youth. 'Who now remembers old Cremorne?' he wrote in nostalgic affection for 'Jullien's grand quadrilles', in which

> With hats on heads and morning coats,
> There footed to his prancing notes
>   Our partner-girls and we.

Jullien's orchestra was a great favourite of the sparkish lads and their girls in the eighteen-sixties. But Cremorne became rowdy and sufficiently disreputable to lose profitable patronage. It was closed in 1877.

Dickens's second London river, the busy harbour, which began beside the City and stretched away past the Pool and Galleon's Reach, is seen in full activity when Mrs Gamp goes to watch the departure of the Antwerp packet (*Martin Chuzzlewit*, chapter 40). It was the 'Ankworks package' to her and not much liked. In the buffeting and confusion of the crowd she cried, 'And I wish it were in Jonadge's belly, I do', confounding the prophet with the whale in her aspiration for a miracle on the Thames.

The Port of London has grown enormously. The navigable channel has been widened and deepened by dredging. Fifty million tons of shipping come in and out every year and here is now the largest and longest of the world's deep-water ports. It is governed by the Port of London Authority, set up in 1909 in order to establish unity of control in place of a medley of separate and competing organisations. The Authority's dominion extends from Teddington upstream away down to the Nore, a distance of seventy miles. The great development of dock-building had begun in 1802 with the West India Dock Company's development of yards between Limehouse and Blackwall. The neighbouring London Docks followed and then on the south bank came the Surrey Docks in 1804, with others in sequence as the need grew.

To the Londoners of the Dickens period the business of the Port was much closer than it is to us. Now that Greater London has overrun the Home Counties and still swallows up increasing miles of farmland with homes for increasing myriads of Londoners, it is easy to forget not only that London has the world's greatest dockland but that it is a harbour at all. The millions travelling underground may never see the working life of the river, and the people of the western, northern, and north-eastern suburbs never cross it in their daily coping with the rush-hour scramble. The Port has its summer trips to Southend and Margate and great liners dock at Tilbury. But it is fair to say that for the average person with an address in Greater London the harbour which feeds his stomach as well as the general prosperity of the town remains scarcely seen and only thought of should a long strike threaten his food supplies. The docker is only noticed when he is not there.

But to the small centralised city of 1830 and 1840, when Dickens was getting his keenest impressions of London life, the harbour was the heart of the town. It was the start of sea travel for the passengers who now leave England from Harwich or the Channel ports or Southampton. The 'Ankworks package' was an example of that. When the journey of escape by river was made in *Great Expectations* (chapter 54), after London Bridge and the Tower had been passed 'we were in among tiers of shipping', says the recounter, Philip Pirrip. 'Here were the Leith, Aberdeen, and Glasgow steamers, loading and unloading goods . . . here were colliers by the score and score, with the coal-whippers plunging off stages on deck, as counterweights to measures of coal swinging up, which were then rattled over the side into barges; here, at her moorings, was to-morrow's steamer for Rotterdam, of which we took good notice; and here tomorrow's for Hamburg.' Some of that traffic remains but it has been overlaid by the mass of greater tonnage. The Londoner does not think of his city as a passenger's port, if he thinks about it as a port at all.

But for Mrs Gamp the Port was at the centre of things. The cabs and chariots drew up with a host of intending voyagers. The steamboats, Dickens wrote,

> lay, alongside of each other—hard and fast for ever to all appearance, but designing to get out somehow, and quite confident of doing it;

The Port of London

and in that faith shoals of passengers and heaps of luggage were proceeding hurriedly on board. Little steamboats dashed up and down the stream incessantly. Tiers upon tiers of vessels, scores of masts, labyrinths of tackle, idle sails, splashing oars, gliding row-boats, lumbering barges, sunken piles, with ugly lodgings for the water-rat within their mud-discoloured nooks; church steeples, warehouses, house roofs, arches, bridges, men and women, children, casks, cranes, boxes, horses, coaches, idlers, and hard-labourers—there they were, all jumbled up together, any summer morning. . . .

In the midst of all this turmoil there was an incessant roar from every packet's funnel, which quite expressed and carried out the uppermost emotion of the scene. They all appeared to be perspiring and bothering themselves exactly as their passengers did; they never left off fretting and chafing, in their own hoarse manner, once.

Such was the second of Dickens's London rivers, this Thames of the mariners and merchandise and of the travellers to Scotland or to Europe, a hard-working Thames with long hours in its docks and wages pitifully low. And low they long remained. In 1889 there was the famous strike for the 'dockers' tanner', sixpence an hour. Yet as an urban presence the early Victorian Port of London seemed to Dickens agreeably urgent, friendly, rich to the eye, and close at hand. Tom Pinch, in the novel quoted, found it so; he enjoyed seeking it out in his walk before going to work in the Temple. He chose 'those parts of the town which were conspicuous for the life and animation pervading them, he became a great frequenter of the market-places, bridges, quays and especially the steamboat wharves: for it was very lively and fresh to see the people hurrying away on their many schemes of business or pleasure and it made Tom glad to think that there was so much change and freedom in the monotonous routine of city lives'.

The third and sinister face of the Thames Dickens had studied at first hand and on very cold nights too. In his account of some vigils in a rowing-boat with the River Police he heard the east wind described as 'a Searcher', but his companions had the stoutest of pea-jackets and he, no doubt, was not considering the foppery with which he has been charged when he selected his overcoat (or coats) for the voyages. At Waterloo Bridge he discussed its suicide aspect with the toll-man who collected the halfpence of those who used it. The bridge was a favourite with would-be enders of unhappy lives and desperate victims of jealousy; in the opinion of this warden of the gate there was 'a deal of jealousy about'. If they jumped off straightforward from the middle of the parapet of the bays of the bridge they did not drown: they were smashed on the buttress. Those who intended a drowning suicide should, said the toll-man, jump from the side of the bay. The Surrey side seemed to be more favoured than the Middlesex, perhaps because there was more poverty and lunacy and lovers' jealousy beyond that bank of the river. It was well to mind how you jumped: it was better to dive. 'There was poor Tom Steele from Dublin. Didn't dive! Bless you, didn't dive at all! Fell down so flat into the water that he broke his breast-bone and lived two days.'

One of the suicides in the novels is that of Betty Higden, the proud penniless woman in *Our Mutual Friend*, who would not go to the workhouse and in her obstinate self-reliance would not be helped privately. She drowned herself upstream near a pleasant Thames-side town where 'you may see the young river, dimpled like a young child, playfully gliding away, unpolluted by the defilements that lie in wait for it'. There she heard the river whispering, 'I am the Relieving Officer appointed by eternal ordinance to do my work. My breast is softer than the pauper-nurse's, death is peacefuller than among the pauper-wards. Come to me!'

Dickens was not at his best, at least to the taste of today, in passages of this kind; it is quoted only as significant of his riverside thoughts. Amid the tranquillity of the first facet of the Thames, the pleasure-seekers' gentle stream, he could still be haunted by the dark aspect of the river he knew so well in all its moods. It was in the Thames above London, the resort of the picnic parties, that Bradley Headstone drowned himself and Rogue Riderhood in a mortal grapple among the icy waters of a winter day.

Down in the Port of London Dickens searched out the ways and means of thieving from ships and barges. I have myself, by courtesy of the River Police, followed in his track on a January night, but far more comfortably. No rowing-boats now for pea-jacketed men, but powerful and cabined motor-boats for the wardens of the Thames. Their beat is now as long as the Port of London territory and so they have seventy miles of water to watch. I was lucky to meet a moon-silvered sky under which to see from the river the sharp ridge of Greenwich Park in noble silhouette with the superb outlines of the Queen's House and the Old Hospital. Closer to the City the huge cranes made their weirdly soaring gestures and the vast warehouses loomed over us like some cliffs of the land of Erebus, through which the classic shades descended into darkness. It was a journey which carried one into the black heart of Dickens's third Thames, the consuming and destroying river.

Recovering the bodies of suicides is still part of the duties of the River Police. Corpse-collecting was once a modestly profitable occupation for the Free Traders in that business. The story of *Our Mutual Friend* begins with Rogue Riderhood engaged on such a prowl and ends with the same scoundrel being himself fished out of the ooze and scum behind one of the rotting lock-gates away upstream, imprisoned in the arms of Bradley Headstone, who finally died as well as killed for love. More of that jealousy, as the Dickensian toll-man would have said. And there was always plenty to steal on and by the water, not only some possible property in the pockets of a person accidentally drowned, which was part of

Riderhood's prey, but the contents of the ships and barges, which could be snatched on dark nights while a sleeping crew was in lazy charge. Barge robbery is still practised and hunted down.

The pea-jacket guide explained to Dickens the assortments of river pillage and the grades of the marauders. The Tier-Rangers lurked in the dark among the tiers of moored vessels, quietly climbed aboard a selected ship, waited for silence or the sound of snores, and then made a swift raid on the sleeping quarters, escaping with any clothes, watches, and cash which could be snatched in a lightning scurry. The Lumpers were men normally engaged in unloading, and occasionally, if a good chance occurred, unloading rather more than their occupation justified. Their special booty was small articles. These could be stuffed into their very large pockets, in which, like clowns in pantomimes, they could conceal packages of surprising sizes. The Lumpers, who had a corps of receivers of stolen goods waiting on shore, did a traffic in smuggled stuff, especially tobacco, using presses to squeeze a single pound into a quite tiny packet. There were more smugglers on a larger scale known as the Truckers, and also there were the Dredgermen, who grabbed property of a not too destructible kind, threw it overboard, and fished it up after the ship had gone while pretending to be dredging coals. A larger exercise in robbery was to cut a barge loose, do the pilfering, and leave it to drift downstream. Nowadays one of the main troubles of the River Police is coping with barges that have broken loose, no doubt accidentally, and are floating about in midstream in the darkness to the great inconvenience and also danger of other tideway traffic.

Farther east were the mud-flats and the marshes, which lingered their clammy covering of mist with a spectral fearsomeness in Dickens's mind. Out in the river were the gruesome hulks, old and decaying men-of-war deemed fit enough to be floating gaols for the carriage of convicts overseas. 'Cribbed and barred and moored by massive rusty chains, the prison-ship seemed in my young eyes to be ironed like the prisoners', was Pip's account in *Great Expectations* of the gaunt vessel looming in the fog. The early chapters of this book have an extraordinary power to make one shiver; the icy damp comes seeping through the words. And just as *Our Mutual Friend* begins and ends with death on the Thames so does the tale of Magwitch the convict start with him plodding, fettered, on a gallant thrust for freedom through the half-frozen swamp and move to his capture, after return from Australia, in the river of the same grey region. Dickens never wrote better of the Thames than when he saw it as a destroyer, fouled by the cruelty of man as much as with the material filth which London's slums and sewers poured into it, to his disgust.

Yet much had altered and even improved before his death. *Great Expectations* was one of the books which he wrote late in his life and dated back to the conditions of his boyhood. The horse-coaches which clatter through it to the market-town had disappeared from the roads and the horror of the hulks had gone from the river. The Thames, which sprawled through the middle of London as it had done in Shakespeare's day, had been put under discipline by embankments, which made the stream narrower and deeper and the mess of mud left by an ebbing tide less conspicuous and less dreary to the eye. The Victoria Embankment, the greatest of Sir Joseph Bazalgette's masterly feats of civil engineering, was built between 1864 and 1870, stretching for a mile and a quarter from Westminster to Blackfriars. This forced the water forward and reclaimed nearly forty acres of squalid foreshore, replacing them with wide roads and public gardens. Here the office-workers may take their midday intervals among well-kept lawns and flower-beds, with occasional music and art exhibitions adjacent. While Dickens was devising the mystery of *Edwin Drood* and setting us the problem which he did not live to resolve, Bazalgette's work was coming to

Progress on the construction of the Thames Embankment at Lambeth, June 1866

its completion. Stone walls, composed of 650,000 cubic feet of granite, with further large masses of brick and concrete, were being imposingly employed to provide the new river bastion and space for a broad high-road from west to east, supplementing the narrow Strand. The Chelsea and Albert Embankments were added soon after. There was thus in the centre of London a new Thames, straitened in its expanse but partly cured of its untidiness.

The early years of the century had seen the coming of new bridges. This began to happen during the childhood of Dickens and before he became a Londoner. Vauxhall Bridge was opened when he was four years old and Rennie's masterpiece of grace, Waterloo Bridge (no longer there), when he was five. The new London Bridge he could, however, watch in the course of its erection. It was opened in 1831 while he was making his way as a reporter. This was Rennie's design; but that supreme bridge architect did not live to see the execution of his plan.

In this way a fourth phase of Dickens's Thames was added to the other three aspects of his waterside philosophy. To the Thames of the pleasure-boats, of the thriving and companionable harbour, and of the sinister and tragic flow there was brought by Bazalgette and his colleagues a substantial riparian dignity. The south bank, between Lambeth and Southwark, remained chaotic. Considered as the central feature of a great capital city, it was, and parts of it still are, shabby and contemptible. In one section of the Surrey shore it has been rescued from its indignity in recent years; whether or not you like the architecture of the Festival Hall it is gay with flags and flowers. The rest of the salvage is long overdue.

Dickens, we know, approved of the Embankment. He would have welcomed the new South Bank between Westminster and Waterloo Bridges and he would especially have enjoyed the illuminations. We are so much accustomed to a town lit up that it is difficult to conceive the darkness of London as he threaded its streets by night. Gas had come in his boyhood. But there was no blaze to counteract the dirt and smokiness of the time when every house had its coal fire and when the mists and fogs hung more densely over a Thames with wide and swampy shores. He would surely have been astonished and elated to see the sweep of the river's bend turned every evening into a crescent of silver that puts a diadem where once was chiefly a disgrace.

CHAPTER TWELVE

Fog and Filth

DICKENS wrote with most power when he was working in the dark. The mist and murk of a riverside scene and the pitchy blackness of his nocturnes are more impressive than his sunlit scenes. By the London fogs he was so disgusted that one feels that he was almost fascinated by the cloak of clammy grime in which they wrapped and almost smothered the town. It has been

A London fog, January 1847

recently maintained that the English climate, though open to plenty of sad and even contemptuous comment, was actually libelled in the novels. A high authority of the British Travel and Holidays Association complained that from the point of view of those who are promoting the tourist industry the work of Dickens has been a positive nuisance and a serious handicap.

But it is nonsense to say that because Dickens had an obsession with fogs and gloom he never permitted the sun to shine. There is, for example, a most encouraging picture of the English summer in *The Old Curiosity Shop*. When Nell and her grandfather make their escape from London to the countryside they are lucky in their weather, tramping on as they are, almost without any luggage or protection against the wind and the rain. They soon reach 'beautiful pastures and fields of corn about which, poised high in the clear blue sky, the lark trilled out her happy song'. We have since been taught that it is the male birds who do the singing and that the poets, including Shakespeare, who have attributed the nightingale's melody to the amorous hen have been inaccurate. Dickens was not a close student of natural history and of botany. He did not stop to distinguish precisely between the various species of warbler or to go into detail about the flowers in the hedgerow. It was enough for him that birds sang and flowers bloomed and that for Nell and the old man 'the air came laden with the fragrance it caught upon its way and the bees, upborne upon its scented breath, hummed forth their drowsy satisfaction as they floated by'.

It is true that the couple ran into rain on the night when they stayed at the Jolly Sandboy, but they had good shelter and a supper of 'tripe, cow-heel, bacon and steak, peas and cauliflowers, new potatoes and sparrow-grass all working up together in one delicious gravy'. Would that the British Travel and Holidays Association could now guarantee such welcome and catering at an English country inn in the middle of the night! The downpour, too, was all for the best since the next morning 'was fine and warm, the ground cool to the feet after the late rain, the hedges gayer and more green, the air clear and everything fresh and healthful'. And so it went on. The sunshine was often streaming in at casement windows and days were 'made for laziness and lying on one's back in green places and staring at the sky till its brightness forced one to shut one's eyes and go to sleep'.

The publicists of the tourist industry in Britain should not be too much depressed by *Bleak House*. There are blue skies in plenty elsewhere in the novels, though one must admit that their radiance is never quite so compellingly described as is that menacing gloom of the fog-bound city. Dr Johnson, who liked long words of Latin origin, once attached the adjective 'inspissated', meaning 'thick', to gloom, and inspissation was never more formidable than in the 'London particular', with filth in the air and filth underfoot, described in the first paragraph of *Bleak House*:

> London. Michaelmas Term lately over, and the Lord Chancellor sitting in Lincoln's Inn Hall. Implacable November weather. As much mud in the streets as if the waters had but newly retired from the face of the earth, and it would not be wonderful to meet a Megalosaurus, forty feet long or so, waddling like an elephantine lizard up Holborn Hill. Smoke lowering down from chimney-pots, making a soft black drizzle, with flakes of soot in it as big as full-grown snow-flakes—gone into mourning, one might imagine, for the death of the sun. Dogs, undistinguishable in mire. Horses, scarcely better—splashed to their very blinkers. Foot passengers, jostling one another's umbrellas, in a general infection of ill-temper, and losing their foothold at street corners, where tens of thousands of other foot passengers have been slipping and sliding since the day broke (if this day ever broke), adding new deposits to the crust upon crust of mud, sticking at those points tenaciously to the pavement, and accumulating at compound interest.
>
> Fog everywhere. Fog up the river, where it flows among green

> aits and meadows; fog down the river, where it rolls defiled among the tiers of shipping and the waterside pollutions of a great (and dirty) city. Fog on the Essex marshes, fog on the Kentish heights. Fog creeping into the cabooses of collier-brigs; fog lying out on the yards and hovering in the rigging of great ships; fog drooping on the gunwales of barges and small boats. Fog in the eyes and throats of ancient Greenwich pensioners, wheezing by the fireside of their wards; fog in the stem and bowl of the afternoon pipe of the wrathful skipper, down in his close cabin; fog cruelly pinching the toes and fingers of his shivering little 'prentice boy on deck. Chance people on the bridges peering over the parapets into a nether sky of fog, with fog all round them, as if they were up in a balloon, and hanging in the misty clouds.

The fog in this book is symbolic as well as actual. Dickens, while he is lamenting the mess and misery of the London streets on a November day, is setting out to denounce the mess and misery caused by an antiquated, dilatory, obstructive, and cruel legal system as typified in the High Court of Chancery. The darkened skies are there as the proper setting for a story of obfuscation in the minds and practices of lawyers. Continually in the novels, whether round the Law Courts or the mud-flats of the river, the fog serves as the stage scenery for sombre and sinister doings.

Mud is no longer a common nuisance on our main roads. The rain slides off their metalled surfaces instead of mixing with dust to make the gluey inspissation which once turned the road into a slippery urban swamp. Such a compost can now be found in undeveloped suburban streets or country lanes; in Dickens's time it was universal and a wet day set Londoners squelching through black slime even in the central thoroughfares. Our motor traffic creates its own nastiness of noise and fumes which the Victorians were spared; but cars do not drop dung, and the droppings of the horse-traffic added to the foulness of the mud as the wheels churned them up. Since animals were then driven along the roads to the

London markets and slaughterhouses instead of being carted there was a further reason for the disgusting condition of the streets in certain parts of the town. The women wore long trailing skirts and the business of getting about without being disgustingly splashed was made the more difficult. In bad weather the man about town wore his spatterdashes, or spats, to protect his boots or shoes. (It will be noticed that in the Dickens world the gentry mainly wore boots and the labourers shoes.) The women, unless they were carriage-folk, protected their feet with pattens, as their overshoes were called.

Some relief was provided for people on foot by the existence of swept crossings. We have our marked places, where the cars must stop to let pedestrians get from one side of the road to another. The Victorians took their chances with the horse-traffic, which could be frightening enough as the private chariots and hired hansoms made all possible speed. These crossings were kept as clean as might be by a man or boy with a broom. He was not as a rule employed by the town council; he was a humble speculator on the chance of collecting enough coppers to keep him meagrely alive.

Naturally *Bleak House*, with its theme of darkness and confusion, had its crossing-sweeper, the boy Jo, who lives in a collapsing slum called Tom-All-Alone's. It is a mass of tumbling tenements pictured in unsparing terms:

> As on the ruined human wretch vermin parasites appear, so these ruined shelters have bred a crowd of foul existence that crawls in and out of gaps in walls and boards; and coils itself to sleep, in maggot numbers, where the rain drips in; and comes and goes, fetching and carrying fever, and sowing more evil in its every footprint than Lord Coodle, and Sir Thomas Doodle, and the Duke of Foodle, and all the fine gentlemen in office, down to Zoodle, shall set right in five hundred years, though born expressly to do it.

'Jo sweeps his crossing all day long'—*Bleak House*

Jo has his broom and his place of work. 'The day changes as it wears itself away, and becomes dark and drizzly. Jo fights it out at his crossing among the mud and wheels, the horses, whips, and umbrellas, and gets but a scanty sum to pay for the unsavoury shelter of Tom-All-Alone's.' In a book whose principal colouring is sepia the existence of the perplexed illiterate half-starved Jo is presented with masterstrokes of anger and of pity. One feels that

Dickens must have sent out for the blackest possible ink in the market. In the century since *Bleak House* was written Jo's broom-work and cadging for coppers have gone. Jo has learned to read and write and look after himself and work for a decent wage. To that reform the fury of Dickens contributed in its own persuasive way, as it was meant to do. But Tom-All-Alone's have not completely disappeared, as any report on housing conditions in the London of today will shamefully reveal.

The fogs remain but they are thinner because less charged with grime. Gas lit the Dickensian streets but neither gas nor electricity warmed the Dickensian homes, which had their coal fires pouring out smoke. On a windless day of heavy cloud the smoke was clamped down on the houses and with its deposit of soot created the filthy layer of fog. By altering our heating-methods to mitigate smoke and especially by creating smokeless zones we have thinned out, but not yet abolished, the plague of fog. Dickens is commonly charged with exaggeration and sometimes, no doubt, in his townscapes he was lavish with the sepia brushwork. But people not so very old can remember a London in which the skies were as pitchy and the streets as muddy as they are painted in the novels, a London in which the crossing-sweeper was still at his brush-work, of a different kind.

The disposal of its dirt and sewage was a problem which London had hardly begun to face when Dickens was a boy and had by no means properly settled when he died. Most readers must be puzzled by the 'mounds' whose value has so much to do with the plot of *Our Mutual Friend*. The mounds were huge piles of dust, ashes, and other refuse which were not municipal dumps but personal property and could be sold at astonishingly high prices, thus earning, or helping to earn, a fortune for John Harman senior and to win for his legatee, Noddy Boffin, the title of 'The Golden Dustman'. Dickens in an article which appeared in *Household*

Words in 1850 stated that the Marylebone dust-heap produced between four and five thousand pounds and that the parish of St George's paid a Mr Stapleton five hundred pounds a year for keeping down its mound by carting the stuff away. So, as the mining prospectors used to say, there was 'gold in them thar hills'.

People are careless and it is always likely that a rubbish-dump will contain a few articles of value worth retrieving by those who can face the filthy task of grubbing in it, as Silas Wegg and Mr Venus actually do in *Our Mutual Friend*. But the main wealth of a mound lay not in such treasure trove but in the ashes, which were useful to brickmakers, and the soot, which was good for manure. Better still for manure was the dung, of human beings as well as of horses and other animals. Dickens was always reticent on the subject of ordure; with him it came under the polite name of 'dust'. But Humphrey House in his very informative book *The Dickens World* reminds us (page 167) of 'the contents of the privies and the piles of mixed dung and ashes which were made in the poorer streets'. Early Victorian London had far more earth-closets and cesspools than water-closets connected with main drainage. So a dust-contractor, to use an evasive name, had an abundance of raw material for his collection and ultimate sale. Humphrey House added that in view of the contents of the mounds 'the idea of Silas Wegg prodding them with his wooden leg becomes almost intolerable', and we may wonder with a shudder what were the contents of the 'scavenger's cart' into which Wegg was finally tipped. But in the story we only get a vague impression of what the mounds contain. Probably there was a sufficiency of real dust and ashes to overlay and obscure the filthier elements.

The rubbish and dirt of London had for centuries been shot into its rivers. We think of London's rivers now as the Thames and Lea, with the Wandle as a small contributor on the Surrey side.

'View of a Dust Yard, from a sketch taken on the spot', about 1840

But it had been a town of many streams. A walker on Hampstead Heath may see the river Fleet in its infancy as a trickle coming out of the Vale of Health pond beside which lived Leigh Hunt, who is generally believed to appear as Harold Skimpole in *Bleak House*. Dickens knew the Heath well and liked to walk there and take a chop at the inn called Jack Straw's Castle or a cup of tea at the Spaniard's Inn Tea-Gardens. The trickle from the Vale of Health works down into the Hampstead Ponds, once part of London's water supply, and it was there that Mr Pickwick, having traced these pools to their sources, found the material wherewith to 'agitate the scientific world with his Theory of Tittlebats'. (Thereby also Keats heard the nightingale which evoked his matchless Ode.) The Fleet then flows away in the direction of King's Cross and swings south to Holborn and the broad hollow of Farringdon Street before it enters the Thames beyond the eastern end of Fleet

Street. It was once navigable as far as Holborn Viaduct and was used by small cargo-boats. But every kind of filth including the effluents of factories and slaughterhouses was poured into it and it had to be covered over and turned into a drain. By 1763 the Fleet, except in its early trickle form, had vanished from sight. It is still an important sewer.

Other rivers included the Tybourne, also coming down from the heights of Hampstead to Bayswater, through which it meandered to the Marble Arch and the site of the Tyburn gallows; the district was known as Tyburnia in Dickens's time. The Walbrook has left its name in the City. On the Surrey side the Peck gave its title to Peckham, and there were two streams with curious names, the Effra, which sounds Celtic and suggests the Welsh Afon (English Avon), and the Neckinger, which ran through Bermondsey to Neckinger Wharf, where Thames pirates were hanged. The name probably came from the hangman's rope, which was known as the Devil's Neckinger.

This stream comes murkily to view at the end of *Oliver Twist* when Bill Sikes takes refuge in the abominable slum called by Dickens Jacob's Island, which had 'every loathsome indication of filth, rot, and garbage on its banks'. The Neckinger remained uncovered at this point for some years after the writing of *Oliver Twist*. An article appearing in the *Morning Chronicle* in September 1849 described it as 'the very capital of cholera', a plague now fortunately banished from England but a prevalent killer in the London of the eighteen-forties. Charles Kingsley visited 'the cholera districts of Bermondsey' in 1849 and related that he saw people 'with no water to drink but that of the common sewer stagnating under their windows, full of dead fish, cats, and dogs'.

It was not only in the poorer districts that sanitation was wholly absent or wretchedly ineffective. The Serpentine in Hyde Park had been created by George II's wife, Queen Caroline, who enjoyed life in a social and decorative way in Kensington Palace, the birthplace of Queen Victoria. The lake of her devising was created by damming the West Bourne, a stream once running down through what is now Westbourne Grove, and by utilising sundry ponds. During early Victorian times a sewer from the north was allowed to run into the Serpentine, whose waters were dangerously fouled. Gases emerged from it, boating-parties were infected, and fevers were spread. Not till 1860 was the sewage diverted and the Serpentine cleansed.

When Lord John Russell became Prime Minister in 1846 he appointed a Sanitary Commission and Henry Austin, who had married Dickens's sister Fanny, was appointed secretary. Austin

A London Park, 1849

thought it his business to look after the family as well as the drains. He made Dickens's brother Alfred one of the new inspectors. A Bill was passed which commanded the provision of a water-closet in every house instead of the usual cesspool outside it; but of course it could not be immediately applied to all existing houses. Dickens wrote about Tom-All-Alone's some years after this legislation, but it is unlikely that sanitary reform had reached that fearsome rookery of the destitute.

Water-closets could not solve the sanitation problem unless they were connected with an efficient system of sewage which would carry the waste well away from London. The early Victorian sewers discharged their contents into the Thames, where the tide sucked the filth downriver and then drove it back to be exposed on the mud-flats or float on the surface of the stream. 'In 1849', wrote Mr Michael Harrison in *London Beneath the Pavement*, 'eighteen thousand died from cholera and in 1854 the deaths numbered twenty thousand. Yet in 1853 the private water-companies were still supplying "drinking" water from the Thames to their customers.'

Reform came. The Metropolitan Water Act of 1852 made filtration compulsory and slowly the water-companies had to alter their ways. The contemporary research of a Yorkshire doctor, John Snow, proved that cholera was caused, at least in part, by drinking contaminated water containing a micro-organism which is lodged and breeds in the human intestines. To read about the water-supply and the sewerage existing in Dickensian London is to discover almost incredible muddle and carelessness. The reforms were gradually but at last effectively made. The Metropolitan Water Board, founded in 1902, supplies and controls the water of Greater London with the exception of Croydon, and does it so successfully that even in dry summers, when other British towns may be harassed by a shortage of supply for their reservoirs, Londoners are not rationed despite the enormous growth of population and enormously increased use of water for industrial as well as domestic purposes. Their water, drawn mainly from the Thames and the Lea, is carefully filtered and one scarcely ever hears of epidemics caused by contamination. The sewers now carry their contents away to 'outfall' stations fairly remote from the city; the sewage is there 'treated' and the remaining 'sludge' taken out to sea and dumped.

The contents of this chapter makes gruesome reading and there is worse to be discovered by the readers of Henry Mayhew's *London Labour and the London Poor,* which was published in 1851. That contains a long section on the sewer-hunters, commonly known as Toshers, who waded up the drains in search of what they could find. Apparently there were numbers of coins and other bits and pieces worth salvage in the sewers, as there were in the mounds. The huge and ferocious sewer-rats had to be driven off and the risk of drowning by a sudden downpour flooding the drains or by an upsurge of tidal water from the Thames had to be met. 'The sewer hunters,' wrote Mayhew, 'occasionally find plate such as spoons, ladles, silver-handled knives and forks, mugs and drinking cups and now and then articles of jewellery. But, even while they are thus in luck, as they call it, they do not hesitate to fill the bags on their backs with the more cumbrous articles they meet with, such as metals of every description, rope and bones.' How all this stuff got into the sewers is puzzling and suggests carelessness on a grand scale. Oddly the Toshers might have been expected to catch mortal diseases but Mayhew reported them to be 'strong, robust, and healthy men generally florid in their complexions, many of them knowing illness only by name'.

The sewer-workers of today, of whom the public hears little, are indispensable public servants; they keep the flow of sewage moving at some physical risk, and if they went on strike for a week and let the drains get clogged London would be a plague city and a great disaster would be inevitable.

Another feature of London life which particularly disgusted Dickens was the condition of the slaughterhouses, especially at Smithfield. This district had become the headquarters of the butchers very early in the history of the City because it was at the end of the Great North Road, down which many flocks and herds were driven to their fate. Originally a suburban district (it was so described in a market charter in the reign of Charles I), it had grown into a centre of teeming population with a consequent prosperity for 'cattle-driving, cattle-slaughtering, bone-crushing, blood-boiling, trotter-scraping, tripe-dressing, paunch-cleaning, gut-spinning, hide-preparing, tallow-melting, and other salubrious proceedings, in the midst of hospitals, churchyards, workhouses, schools, infirmaries, refuges, dwellings, provision-shops, nurseries, sick-beds, every stage and baiting-place in the journey from birth to death'.

As a result, Dickens said, 'into the imperfect sewers of this City you have the immense mass of corruption, engendered by these practices, lazily thrown out of sight to rise in poisonous gases into your house at night when your sleeping children will most readily absorb them and to find its languid way at last into the river that you drink.' This background to 'the jolly old English roast beef' was contrasted with the far better organisation and more humane methods practised in the *abattoirs* of Paris, of which Dickens made a special personal survey. Extremely pro-French in many matters, especially where food and drink were concerned, he made a damning comparison of the slaughterhouse arrangements in the two capitals. One might not nowadays expect France to be far ahead of England in cleanliness and avoidance of cruelty, but Dickens found it so, and his essay, ironically called 'A Monument of French Folly' and to be found in his *Reprinted Pieces*, is a withering attack on the scandal of Smithfield and similar places in his time.

Dickens and Mayhew provide a revolting survey of London's filthy habits. But we can at least congratulate ourselves on a fairly happy ending, although the problem of sewage disposal at seaside towns with growing populations is a grave one and has to be expensively met if beaches are not to be fouled. The London of the mounds, of the cesspools, which were often close enough to the wells to infect them, and of the Thames regarded as a major drain, has gone. It was gradually cleaned up by the work of reformers such as Sir Edwin Chadwick, whose *Report on the Sanitary Condition of the Labouring Population of Great Britain* appeared in 1842, three years after Dickens had described Jacob's Island in *Oliver Twist.* Chadwick's researches and recommendations had their results in the reforms initiated by Sir Robert Peel's Government and continued by others, and Mayhew's book was a further stimulus to the general cleaning up which was put slowly but effectively in hand during subsequent decades.

The drafting of reforms had to be carried out and the reforms themselves enacted by politicians with Civil Servants behind them to execute their policies. On both of these classes Dickens poured much contempt, often in a very amusing way. He had, however, powerfully assisted their work by his incomparably vivid pictures of the ugliest side of urban life. The vast popularity of his books was bound to break through public ignorance of the sickening conditions in which many were living and to overcome the deplorable apathy about scandals, which could be remedied by resolute action against the sloth and misrule of boards and councils and the greed of vested interests. The myriads of readers first turned to Dickens for a good story; in the process their consciences were given a nasty jolt, which had excellent results in creating a public opinion supporting the essential legislation.

CHAPTER THIRTEEN

The American Scene

DICKENS had the good fortune to live in an age when a great author was accepted as a great man and an asset to his country and the world. Writers could receive, sometimes to a harassing extent, the salutations, even the worship, now lavished upon film-stars whose face is their fortune for a year or two and financially a very large fortune too. In payment, too, authors could then do astonishingly well. No publisher today would offer a substantial fee for a book of essays by an unknown youngster; few want a book of essays even by an author of standing. Macrone put down one hundred and fifty pounds for the Boz *Sketches*. As Mr Priestley has written, 'This is worth mentioning, if only because too many people assume that young authors are much better off than they were when Dickens was young. But one hundred and fifty pounds in 1836 would buy as much as one thousand pounds will buy in 1961.' Between the years 1815 and 1842 there was no income-tax and when revived by Peel in the latter year it was sevenpence in the pound.

Dickens, for a while at least, enjoyed the acclamation and the social triumphs. Not many writers shrink coyly away from high praise and laurel wreaths. The man who says that he cannot endure flattery and really means it is a rarity. When Dickens visited America in 1842 he discovered that an author could have the status of a theatrical luminary (his friend Macready had no such tumultuous reception) and the plaudits usually awaiting a conquering hero in war and nowadays in space-travel. The country 'rose at him', as they say of wildly enthusiastic audiences in a playhouse or a concert-hall.

It was not his first experience of the cheers and the honours. His early work had been widely translated and applauded from republican America to imperial Russia. In 1842 he had only published six books, *Sketches by Boz*, *The Pickwick Papers*, *Oliver Twist*, *Nicholas Nickleby*, *The Old Curiosity Shop*, and *Barnaby Rudge*. The best was still to come. But he already stood on the summits of popularity.

We are accustomed to think of the Scots as cautious in judgment and unlikely to be effusive and even gushing in praise. The great Edinburgh critics and men of law were hard of head. But it was Little Nell of *The Old Curiosity Shop*, the mothering child and the Wendy of her day (a type to be followed up in Florence Dombey and Little Dorrit), who drove into the heads and hearts of Edinburgh. Nell has ceased to be a favourite and the account of her death now receives such slangy dismissals as 'sob-stuff' and 'a tear-jerker'. But the literary as well as legal judge, Lord Jeffrey, founder of the severe *Edinburgh Review*, was a devoted admirer of Dickens and especially of his Nell. Scotland was ahead of England in bestowing its highest civic honours on the young man, who received the Freedom of the City of Edinburgh in 1841, only seven years after he had been there as an unknown journalist in the workaday routine of a speedy and trusted shorthand reporter.

America was already eager to see and lionise him, bubbling over with what he called 'enthoosymoosy', and he was no less eager to see America. Stiffly conservative opinion in England might continue to think of it as a land of rebellious colonials who should have been 'Put Down' and, alas, were not. 'Putting Down' people and things was the chief and perhaps the only notion of that crush-them-all Tory, Alderman Cute in *The Chimes*. ('There's a certain amount of cant in vogue about Starvation and I mean to Put It Down.') If the Alderman had discussed America as well as the impudent English poor who were so audacious as to dislike starvation he would have demanded that America be Put Down—at the bottom of the Atlantic.

But to the British Radicals here was a land of hope and freedom, of endeavour and enterprise. They were critical of and in some cases sourly hostile to monarchy and here was a young and confident republic. It was, they believed, free from all dominance of class. Its Government did not belong, as though by prescriptive right, to the Coodles and Doodles and Foodles so loathed by Dickens. It was the home of refugees from oppression and, especially in the case of the Irish, from tyrannical landlords, hunger, and privation. Dickens could be as cynical as any practitioner of what America was to call 'debunking' and none turned a sharper eye on the shams of supposed democracy. But America was unseen and he could sail away to observe the republic in action with more hope of a heartening experience than fear of a melancholy disillusion. It had given him lavish encouragement and on his landing it provided, even more than it had promised, an overwhelming generosity of welcome.

Moreover, there was an emerging literature of the republic and there were its leaders to meet when he landed in Boston. Emerson, just reaching forty, had been to England and had made a close friendship with Thomas Carlyle. He was renowned as a leader of Transcendentalism; the word baffled Dickens, who on inquiring learned that its devotees 'are followers of my friend, Mr Carlyle'. The dictionary defines the members of this school as the disciples 'of exalted thought and language' and also as extravagant idealists, people unlikely to appeal to the practical realistic Dickens with his feet on the ground and his head rarely in the clouds. He found, however, in Emerson's essays not only 'much that is fanciful and dreamy' but 'much more that is true and manly, honest and bold'. So he politely decided that, though the Transcendentalists had their vagaries, because of their 'hearty disgust of Cant' he would be one of their company if he were a Bostonian. Another of his welcomers was Oliver Wendell Holmes, then practising as a doctor but deeply interested in poetry and literature of all kinds. In New York Dickens met Edgar Allan Poe, who wanted an outlet for his stories in England and was kindly given some introductions which proved fruitless for the time being. Their temperaments were contrasted and there seems to have been no mutual liking.

A friendship with Longfellow was begun and this was to be continued with warm hospitality in England. Hawthorne was not one of the Dickens enthusiasts; he was suspicious of English visitors and apprehensive of superior attitudes and denigrating remarks. Walt Whitman was still a youngster variously employed in and around New York. His emergence as a man and a poet who shattered the conventions of poetical form and of reticence about sex occurred a dozen years later. Dickens, with his political Radicalism, would have welcomed some of Whitman's trumpeting on freedom's side. But with his conservatism as to what might decently be said he could have been painfully shocked by the frankness of the American's freedom of speech.

The man whom he most wanted to meet was Washington Irving, the much-travelled author and diplomat who had been attached to the American Embassy in London from 1829 to 1832. He had travelled widely and like Boz he wrote his *Sketch-Books*. He had called on Walter Scott at Abbotsford, and later, when back in America, he had sent letters of high praise to Dickens as the latter's books appeared. In a reply made at the end of 1841 Dickens had said, 'There is no living writer, and there are very few among the dead, whose approbation I should feel so proud to earn. And with everything you have written upon my shelves, and in my thoughts, and in my heart of hearts, I may honestly and truly say so.' Here would be a most congenial meeting, and when it came it was certainly not one of Dickens's American disappointments. 'What pleasure I have had in seeing and talking with you I will not attempt to say. I shall not forget it as long as I live.' That was written two months after Dickens had landed in America in 1842.

Washington Irving

The clamorous reception naturally gratified Dickens immensely for a while but it was inevitably exhausting. Invitations poured in. To be thus fêted was soon, even for so young and active a man, to be fretted and fatigued. His wife had never wanted to come with him; she would rather have stayed at home with her four young children, who had to be left in the charge of others. Being lioness to the lion of the applauding crowds was a part for which she had neither aptitude nor appetite. Dickens, though at first he relished the cheering and the compliments, began to feel the strain; he was an impulsive quick-tempered man, easily put on edge, and tact was not his strong point.

He had arrived in high spirits but also with a grievance. It was a grievance well justified. He had won myriads of American readers and no American rewards. His books had been pirated by publishers, who exploited the absence of a copyright convention. It was a form of robbery which continued for many years after Dickens's death. The American authors knew it to be a scandal and if Dickens had conferred with them and with the editors of the more responsible papers, who were on his side, and made his protest through them, he might not have achieved his end but he would have effectively started his campaign in the right way. But he chose a banquet in his honour to make a stinging attack on the pillage of his work, when all that was expected was a speech of eloquent thanks for his reception, a tribute to American hospitality, and some acceptable and conventional sentiments phrased with Dickensian felicity.

There was undoubtedly a latent sense of guilt about literary theft, and for a guest to prick in public the uneasy conscience of his host may be courageous but is not tactics. Most of the American press took its freedom to be an excuse for fierce hard-hitting and jeering scurrility. The *New York Times* was on his side but the lesser dogs were at once snapping at his heels and doing all they could to bite as well as bark. So began that breach of sympathy in higher quarters and rank animosity in lower ones which was to produce the satirical picture of America in *Martin Chuzzlewit*. This, the next of his great novels, is much enlivened in its middle reaches by the grotesquely amusing figures of such ridiculous Americans as Major Hannibal Chollop, the Honourable Elijah Pogram, Member of Congress, and the anti-British orators who were determined to twist the Lion's tail and let the world know it. It was a savage mockery which Dickens tried later to justify by stating that some of his ridicule was based on 'a literal paraphrase of public proceedings in the United States (especially the proceedings of a certain Brandywine Association), as printed in the London *Times*, whose files could be referred to'. But the whole tone of this attack could only inflame those Americans whom he had already angered and *Martin Chuzzlewit* was publicly burned in New York, a sad sequel to that first outburst of 'enthoosymoosy' which had greeted his arrival in Boston.

There was bound to be anti-British feeling in the America he had entered. The war which won independence was only two generations away and the Anglo-American War of 1812–14 was less than thirty years distant. During that futile contest a British army had captured Washington in August 1814 and burned the White House. Although the campaign was abortive and the war ended indecisively, the Americans could not be expected immediately to forget the presence of British troops on their soil for the second time and the occupation, with arson, of their capital. Such memories, like the buildings, burn. Furthermore, the country when Dickens visited it, was torn by political disputes. The annexation of Texas was a matter of bitter controversy in which President Tyler was defied by the Senate. It is little wonder that when Dickens was received by the President he found that 'he looked somewhat worn and anxious, and well he might, being at war with everybody—but the expression of his face was mild and pleasant and his manner was remarkably unaffected, gentlemanly, and agreeable'.

On leaving Boston Dickens visited New York, Philadelphia, Baltimore, Washington, Pittsburgh, and St Louis and penetrated as far south as Virginia; he also went out into the prairie country of the Middle West. He found the rooms and the trains (in railway development America was ahead of England) oppressively heated. As an Englishman Dickens was used to cold rooms and the Americans had learned to stoke up. 'The fault common to all American interiors', he wrote, 'is the presence of the eternal, accursed, suffocating, red-hot demon of a stove, whose breath would blight the purest air under Heaven.' Disagreement about the proper temperature of a room is as much a cause of international friction as are political and economical disputes. The tiring Dickens was overheated in temper as in body and another cause of fury was the amount of tobacco-chewing and spitting. That was unpleasant and even disgusting, but it hardly called for such constant rancour as it evoked. Much of the journeys were made by canal and river and the voyages were often agreeable. 'There was much in this mode of travelling', was his verdict, 'which I heartily enjoyed at the time and looked back upon with great pleasure.'

The *American Notes* were written immediately on his return to Britain. They are not in fact so anti-American as some have thought them. Of course Dickens was revolted by the continuance of slavery and lashed its supporters with all the vehemence at his command, but he found a great deal to approve and commend. He was impressed, for example, by a general courtesy to women which was not so common in England. At a meal on a canal-boat he noticed some unmannerly and ravenous attack on the victuals by the males but 'no man sat down until all the ladies were seated or omitted any little act of politeness which could contribute to their comfort. Nor did I ever once, on any occasion anywhere, during my rambles in America, see a woman submitted to the slightest act of rudeness, incivility, or even inattention.' No doubt Mrs Dickens appreciated that, but there is very little said of her endurances and approvals or disapprovals during the long and tiring journeys made. She was used to being treated as the appendage of a great man. She was accustomed to that role and probably said little. He could abundantly do the talking.

Another subject of praise was the universities. He found the resident professors at the University of Cambridge (Harvard) to be

> gentlemen of learning and varied attainments and without one exception that I can call to mind men who would shed a grace upon and do honour to any society in the civilised world. . . . Whatever the defects of the American Universities may be they disseminate no prejudices; rear no bigots; dig up the buried ashes of no old superstitions; never interpose between the people and their improvement; exclude no man because of his religious opinions; above all, in their whole course of study and instruction, recognise a world, and a broad one, lying beyond the college walls.

He went on to praise the humanising effect of the University on Boston, where it created valuable friendships and dispelled vanity and prejudice. At Boston, he claimed, 'the almighty dollar sinks into something comparatively insignificant, amid a whole Pantheon of better gods'. This was a side-slap at the old English universities with their rigid clericalism and religious tests. Isolated in their own enclaves of classical scholarship and often of laziness, they were not recognising the outside world and its demands on education. Dickens on his way to New York did not stop at New Haven and visit Yale, where early in the nineteenth century there had been pioneer work in the teaching of science. His opinions of Yale's utility and good qualities might have been the same.

New York he found to be not so clean and trim as Boston and altogether less developed as a city. It was more bustling, more international. New England had deserved that English name in many ways; here in New York was the beginning of New Cosmopolis. But there were primitive conditions. Pigs were wandering about Broadway. 'They are the city scavengers, these pigs . . . never attended upon or fed or driven or caught . . . just as evening is closing in you will see them roaming towards bed by scores, eating their way to the last.' The shops, dotted with bright jets of gas, reminded him of Oxford Street and Piccadilly. Broadway now means to most the bright lights of entertainment, but New York then was relying chiefly on its bars and skittle-alleys for fun and games. There were two large theatres, the Park and the Bowery, which Dickens described 'as generally deserted', and the Olympia, a tiny show-box for vaudevilles and burlesques, which a popular comedian called Mitchell managed to fill. There was also Niblo's Garden, a summer theatre, which was suffering from the general depression. Broadway was soon to change its face and put on a garish splendour.

It is typical of Dickens's obsession by prisons that he gave

View of New York from Weehawken, 1839

special attention to the American gaols and also to asylums, hospitals, and reformatories. His observations on these occupy a very large portion of *American Notes*. In Boston there was much to praise, intelligent and humane treatment of the blind, and no less sensible provision for the insane. In the case of the latter he could see that 'moral influence' was far more efficacious as a means of restraint and as a method of cure than all the strait-waistcoats and fetters used elsewhere at the time in ignorance and cruelty. 'It is obvious', he concluded, 'that one great feature of the system is the inculcation and encouragement, even among such unhappy persons, of a decent self-respect.' The same excellence he discovered in the treatment of the old paupers and young offenders against the law. The Boston House of Correction he also approved for its working arrangements and reasonable discipline. But the Tombs Prison and the Lunatic Asylum in New York depressed him greatly. At the prison in Philadelphia the system of solitary confinement, which was introduced in London as a great reform by the creation of Pentonville with separate cells in 1842, was in practice and held to be enlightened. But Dickens, while convinced that it was meant for humanity and reformation of character, decided that 'the benevolent gentlemen who carry it into execution do not know what they are doing'. The solitude seemed to him to cause 'acute and tremendous anguish' and to render the prisoner morally and mentally warped and 'unfit for rejoining the busy contacts of the world'. It was burial alive, and that was the view of England's John Galsworthy seventy years later as expressed in his play *Justice*, which vividly and poignantly showed the torture of solitude in the cells.

The spoils system whereby many public appointments change hands according to the sway of party politics, with members of the victorious party replacing the members of the defeated one, was at work even in the government of a lunatic asylum. Thus an intelligent man who had learned to be an efficient administrator could be turned out as the result of a political election held on issues wholly remote from the running of a prison or a mental hospital. When one side went out at Washington and the other came in it was a case of 'the jobs for the boys' even though the job might be one of a specialised kind and with no political connection whatever.

America to Dickens was cursed and corrupted by this party spirit 'sickening and blighting everything of wholesome life within its reach'. At Washington, while he admired the President, he detested and despised most of the Members of Congress, in which assembly he was revolted by 'Dishonest Faction in its most depraved and unblushing form, staring out from every corner of the crowded hall'. Yet he admitted that there were there men of high integrity and undoubted abilities. What continually infected American public life, in his opinion, was the poison of the unscrupulous newspapers, which were under no effective check of laws against libel and so made the foulest attacks on any whom the proprietors and editors wished to discredit. He suffered himself in this way and saw others suffer too.

But with the exception of slavery and book piracy there were no social faults attacked in *American Notes* which Dickens had not already attacked and would continue to attack quite as forcibly in his own country. He criticised 'smart' finance in his summary of the American scene, but he had only recently exposed without mercy the City sharks of London in *Nicholas Nickleby*. He had written of wretched slums in New York but they did not exceed in squalor and in menace to public health the Jacob's Island of *Oliver Twist*. If the Tombs in New York was a dungeon of despair it was no worse than the Newgate which he had described in his Boz days. In matters of cleanliness and medical care he found no American parallel to Mrs Gamp, the slatternly and alcoholic midwife in *Martin Chuzzlewit*.

An absurd kind of American humbug, vanity, and patriotic boasting is ridiculed in that book, but it also contained the very English Pecksniff, a ludicrous and monstrous vessel of cant and self-seeking. Podsnap in *Our Mutual Friend* is as ludicrous a specimen of national bigotry and pride as any of the American ranters whom he cartooned. Dickens was impressed by the Unitarians of Boston and said little of religious hypocrisy in America, whereas he continued to portray its most odious English types such as Stiggins, Chadband, and the Howlers in the chapels. English politics he mocked from the Eatanswill election in *The Pickwick Papers* to the arrival in Parliament of Mr Veneering in *Our Mutual Friend*. He found the society of the Boston intellectuals at least as well informed and well graced as any in London. There was really no occasion for all the anger that he caused.

The more sensible Americans had not been offended and remained his champions. They did not hold the sentimental view that an attractive young author should also be an unworldly idealist with a soul soaring above money and quite unconcerned about his copyrights. They knew where Dickens was right. Longfellow said that the *American Notes* were 'severe, but good-natured' and the section on slavery 'grand'.

In 1867 Dickens returned to America with some natural trepidation and an equally natural curiosity. It was a largely altered America. The Civil War had strained the country's energy and resources and had bled the nation to an appalling extent with its loss of half a million young and vigorous lives. The greatest man in political life, President Lincoln, had been murdered and his successor, Andrew Johnson, who received Dickens in Washington, was living a harassed life. Slavery had gone with the Thirteenth Amendment to the Constitution, but that did not mean a quick settlement and willing composition with the South, and tempers were high. Dickens was visiting a country still passionately divided, but he was not now travelling as a candid critic or political commentator. He was there as a performer and as a performer he conquered.

Having perfected his dramatic technique in the readings of episodes from his novels and made himself a master of their presentation, he was invited and most willing to show his dramatic flair and fire on American platforms. The financial prospects were excellent. He had fears of a hostile reception but these were immediately proved groundless. There was more than admiration for the histrionics of the readings. There was friendship in abundance. The difficulty was not to draw the crowds in but to find room for them when he gave the readings. At Harvard the undergraduates, striving to get places, were frustrated because speculators had bought up all the seats and were selling them at very high prices. He met many old acquaintances, but not Washington Irving, who had died in 1859. It was a triumph and one of time's revenges was his entertainment to a grand dinner in New York at which the hosts were his old enemies, the American press. The copyright question had not been solved but he did not press the point, and in his speech of reply at the dinner warmly complimented America on its many advances in its way of living and stressed the essential unity of the two peoples. No disaster could be worse than separation and enmity. Better for this earth to be fired by a comet than that the two great nations, 'each of which has, in its own way and hour, striven so hard and so successfully for freedom, should ever again be arrayed against one another'.

It had been a triumph, with the 'enthoosymoosy', which had been lost, fully regained. Dickens, who jokingly spoke of himself as 'The Inimitable', had once more proved the truth of the adjective. But this time the triumph was even more of an ordeal. The dramatic recitals with himself as solo actor had been so exhausting in England that his friends had warned him to be careful. He was an ageing man. We do not now think of fifty-five years as more than arrival in life's middle span but people then wore themselves out quickly. (Macaulay died at fifty-nine and Thackeray at fifty-two.) Dickens had to get through his performances with long rests and very little food. He took stimulants before them and sedatives after them in order to keep his energy and then get some sleep. When he returned to England he had only two more years to live, and we may suspect that the second sampling of the American scene had contributed to the height of his blood-pressure and the fatal stroke in 1870. But he had put things right and now America had agreed that in the strictures of his *American Notes* he had never been far wrong and that in the approvals of many American institutions and practices he had shown more true appreciation than his critics had troubled to notice.

CHAPTER FOURTEEN

Christmas

THERE is much darkness in the world about which Dickens wrote. This murkiness and muddle in the ways of life he did his best to dispel, but he never pretended that it was a transient darkness preceding an inevitable dawn. Accordingly, in a book about the conditions and events of his time it may be more agreeable to end with one subject in which he found abiding warmth and light, namely Christmas. There is an additional reason for doing so in the tendency of recent commentators on the work of Dickens to concentrate on his unhappiness, the break-up of his marriage, in which he was probably much to blame, his effort to find consolation through another and concealed attachment, and the strains on nerve and physique of one who had continually pressed himself too hard in the bustle and fervour of an overcrowded life.

It is not the present purpose to analyse the personal frets and frustrations impairing the happiness which should have flowed from an externally triumphant career. It is obvious that Dickens looked deeper into the sickness of Victorian society as he grew older, that the colour-scheme of his writing became more sombre, and that the bubbling gaiety which filled his early stories with comic characters who were, as we say, 'out of this world' lost its effervescence. That malaise is one matter; the background of the books and the scenes in which he set his characters is another. Thus any public events or social customs and rituals which were around him when he wrote must be of interest to his readers. Amid the many causes of his anger was one special cause for an escape into exhilaration. That was the observance of Christmas.

Dickens enjoyed Christmas, and when he enjoyed a thing, as when he hated a thing, he did so with all his heart and at the top of his voice. His Christianity was of a highly emotional kind and his zest for the midwinter festival had little to do with theology. Pity and generosity were strong in him and now was the time for mercy and for giving. He was an extravagant man not only in his flow of soul but in the flow of money too. Now was the right time to be cheerfully spendthrift and to give, not by signing cheques for organised charities and foreign missions, but by handing over a gift without any niggling inquiries about the deserts of the recipient. He liked a feast as the proper contrast to a fast. At Christmas even the hungriest had a chance to be less hungry and the chilliest could manage to stoke up some kind of fire. The glowing hearth behind the shuttered windows was always in his mind when he wrote of Christmas. Even his wealthy characters had no central heating and one cannot imagine Dickens welcoming the feast by putting a match to a gas fire. If the poor lacked the seasonal flame and fuel they must be helped to the kindling. And the table must be loaded. The Dickens novels are richly savoured with the pleasures of 'a good tuck-in'. To church first, for the hymns, not the sermon, but certainly to the punch-bowl and the steaming roast thereafter.

Compassion for deprived children was dominant always in his thoughts and sympathies. He was never a man to put away childish things. The oldest traditions of Christmas merrymaking included dressing up and masquerade, a tradition in which he revelled. He was devoted to acting of a serious kind and also to the lighter miming of charades and all kinds of family nonsense. A skilful conjurer, he was glad to show his nimbleness in sleight of hand. He had a large family and enjoyed giving large parties. Christmas called for 'keeping open house', as people used to call a ready hospitality. Those who took pot luck with him found plenty in the pot.

But we get things out of proportion if we think of Dickens as obsessed by Christmas. Unfortunately because of a few things that he wrote, a very small portion of his total work, the phrase 'a regular Dickens Christmas' has become lodged in the general mind. Some people, who may have read very little of that vast output, talk of Dickens as though he were a perpetual Santa Claus, forever chortling amid a forest of Christmas trees and unable to sit at his desk without the chimes in his ears and the carol-singers at the door. In fact he did not write much about Christmas, but what he did write was such a powerful compost of convivial gaiety and deep compassion for those who had small chance to be gay that it made a tremendous impact on his readers.

In his first book, the *Sketches by Boz*, in which the most sinister sides and depths of London life were unsparingly described, there is one essay on Christmas dinners. The cells at Newgate get far more space and attention than the turkey and plum pudding. In *The Pickwick Papers* there is much more about the loathsome conditions of the debtors in the Fleet Prison than about the Christmas junketings at Dingley Dell, which have been so much remembered. When he was an established author he wrote a long short story called *A Christmas Carol* which was so vivid and so agreeable to Victorian taste that it was widely dramatised and continued to be eagerly read all over the world, with the result that the name of Scrooge, the converted skinflint, was imbedded in the English language as a symbol of all such parsimony. Naturally the success had to be followed up for the Dickens family was increasing and there were hard-up relatives to help. Hence came *The Chimes*, which at first sold better than *A Christmas Carol*, and *The Cricket on the Hearth*. The better part of *The Chimes*, at least for the readers of today, is the sharp fun poked at the Malthusian economists with their dread of surplus population, and at the tyrannical alderman who believes that everything distasteful to him, including most of the population, should be 'Put Down'. It is a pity that the biting edge of comedy in *The Chimes* is less prominent than the visions in the belfry, which are a bore.

The volume of collected pieces called *Christmas Stories* only carried that title because they were written for the Christmas numbers of *Household Words*, the magazine to whose editing Dickens gave a large amount of time and serious attention, using it for the expression of Radical opinions about reform as well as for the kind of fiction which is written simply to entertain. This volume contains two short essays on Christmas topics, of which the second, called 'What Christmas is as we Grow Older', strikes a melancholy and mournful note since it makes remembering the dead a principal Christmas duty. It contains an allusion to the writer's young sister-in-law, Mary Hogarth, to whom he was intensely devoted. At the age of seventeen she had made 'a mourning Christmas in a house of joy' and Dickens called on himself 'to look upon her now'. His Yule was not all rollicking by the hearth. 'Lost friend, lost child, lost parent, sister, brother, wife, we will not discard you. You shall hold your cherished places in our Christmas hearts and by our Christmas fires; and in the season of immortal hope, and on the birthday of immortal mercy, we shall shut out nothing!'

In the rest of this fairly large assembly of stories some have a passing reference to Christmas and most no reference at all. Only intermittently do they represent Dickens at his best. The two pieces on Mrs Lirriper and her Lodgings and her Legacy should not be missed, as they may be since the book is not widely read on the scale of the great novels. Mrs Lirriper is a gossiping landlady with a soft heart and a sharp tongue whose shapeless prattle is as racy as that of Mrs Gamp or Flora Finching. She is what Sean O'Casey would call 'a darrlin' gab', product of the Dickens genius and not of the Dickens Christmas. She certainly must not be shut out. In the major books Christmas is not a constant intruder, only intervening as that season naturally intervenes once in twelve months in all our lives. If it does it serves a purpose, as when the boy Pip in *Great Expectations* is miserably hugging his dangerous secret amid the jollities of the Gargery Christmas table. The idea of Dickens continually rolling out the barrel and lighting up the Christmas tree is unjust to one so constantly concerned with the cruelty of man to man and especially of man to child, with the fog of the law and the filth of its prisons, and with all the black shapes of pestilent poverty and the fever-breeding slums. Such haunting presences recur far more often than do the candles and the tinsel and the exuberant hilarity of 'the regular Dickens Christmas'.

The December feast had acquired a growing and expanding celebration during the early part of the nineteenth century, and that was to be intensified. During the whole of Dickens's lifetime Christmas was of short duration since there was no Boxing Day bank holiday and people were back at work on 26 December, a shocking idea to those whose break now often spreads over four days with the aid of Saturday and Sunday. If Dickens enjoyed the habit of sending Christmas cards, a business which children properly enjoy but which has swollen oppressively for adults in our own time, he could not have done so until he was approaching middle age since Christmas cards were only introduced in 1846. A founder of the custom was Sir Henry Cole, who was a distinguished member of a profession rarely approved by Dickens, the Civil Service. It may be doubted whether the Tite Barnacles followed Sir Henry's lead, but they could have had a card designed with a cluster of molluscs on a family tree. Sir Henry's card, which was to be the ancestor of such a swarming progeny, showed a convivial and well-to-do domestic group with the poor on the edges in receipt of gifts.

Christmas crackers were a product of the eighteen-fifties and therefore unknown to Dickens in his childhood and to his elder

The first Christmas card

children in their younger years. So, judged by our exacting standards of all that has to be bought and planned, kept in mind, and parcelled and posted during the previous weeks, the Dickens Christmas of one day was a mere trifle. The pressure of Christmas salesmanship with catalogues arriving in the autumn is something that he never knew. This he might have thought with some reason to be more in the interests of one of Mr Merdle's joint-stock companies than of the true spirit of the season.

Not only was the early and mid-Victorian Christmas much shorter than ours: it also had its active enemies. The extreme Protestants viewed the word with suspicion and even dislike. Its second syllable had a Romish look; might not all this feasting be part of a Papist plot? This apprehension has survived in Scotland with only a gradually diminishing strength and the day of the Nativity is still not a legally appointed holiday north of the Border. Pre-Reformation Scotland had lit the Yule fires and greeted the midwinter, after which the days would happily lengthen, with long and lavish rejoicings lasting from 18 December to 7 January, during which time malefactors could claim rights of sanctuary. The rites of fire and feast remain in the Up-Helly-Aa of the Shetlanders.

But the impact of the Reformation was particularly powerful in Scotland and such customs were put down as pagan survivals, which indeed some of them were, or as Roman practices and contrary to the bleak creed of the Calvinists. The anti-Christmas feeling continued to be held with a passionate austerity by many Scottish Presbyterians, and the English Evangelicals and Dissenters were also long reluctant to let cheerfulness break in. It is probable that a humbug like Pastor Stiggins took the chance to increase his swilling of pineapple rum, but unlikely that Melchizedek Howler ceased because of Christmas to howl about the wrath to come. One English man of letters, Sir Edmund Gosse, brought up in an extremely Puritanical Victorian household, has related his father's hatred of the very word, which he pronounced as though tasting poison. He insisted that there be no Christmas observance and no special Christmas dishes served in a family which was not to be contaminated by heathen or Roman habits. To cook a plum pudding was the Devil's work in his opinion; finding one in the home he threw it on the fire.

But among even the sternest Protestants in England there has been a growing recognition that to keep Christmas cordially is at least a pardonable weakness. Decorating the house with branches at midwinter was a very old habit and probably dates back into pre-Christian times and the pagan rites of tree-worship. The practice was surrounded with superstitious fears; to leave the garlands on the wall when the Twelve Days of the medieval Christmas, whose festal quality survived the Reformation in England, had passed was to risk the worst of luck. Robert Herrick, the far from austere Devonshire parson, recorded the proper procedure for bedecking and then stripping a home in the seventeenth century:

> Down with the rosemary and so
> Down with the bays and mistletoe;
> Down with the holly, ivy, all
> Wherewith ye dressed the Christmas Hall:
> That so the superstitious find
> No one least branch there left behind:
> For look, how many leaves there be
> Neglected there (maids, trust to me)
> So many Goblins you shall see.

Rosemary, whose name means 'dew of the sea', was once a Christmas favourite and was used not only on the walls but as a garnish for dishes, including the boar's head commonly expected on the Yuletide table. A poet who wrote of Christmas soon after Herrick gave this command:

> Then, if you would send up the Brawner's head,
> Sweet Rosemary and Bays around it spread;
> His foaming tusks let some large Pippin grace
> Or midst these thund'ring Spears an Orange place.

Mistletoe was suspected by some of being an evil relic of the ancient unchristian Britons and their Druidical rites, but it has held its place among the Christmas garlands, as rosemary has not.

The chief dishes for a Dickens dinner were turkey, plum pudding, and mince pies with a goose for those who could only afford that—and how Bob Cratchit managed to afford a goose out of the fifteen shillings a week that Scrooge paid him to keep a home and family fed, warmed, and clothed is difficult to understand. But it was a small goose and described as a bargain, and finished at a sitting. Joe Gargery, who had some formidable and voracious guests, provided no turkey or goose but two roast stuffed fowls and a leg of pickled pork.

Much has been made of the Christmas which Mr Pickwick and his companions enjoyed, with the unquenchable hospitality of Mr Wardle, at Dingley Dell. The fact is that the revels were those of a wedding two days before Christmas and not of Christmas Day itself, whose celebration is curtly dismissed. The twenty-third of December had its marriage and a wedding breakfast at midday with plenty to eat and more to drink. Then comes the astounding mention of 'a twenty-five mile walk undertaken by all the males at the host's suggestion'. The purpose was 'to get rid of the wine'. Did Mr Wardle take that gigantic piece of exercise himself or was he praying for a little peace in his home and a quiet nap? That the wedding-breakfasted and well-wined males would after midday have cared to or tried to stumble for some eight hours along the frozen roads and through the snowdrifts mentioned is unlikely. That they contrived to cover twenty-five miles without total collapse is unthinkable. Even had they achieved three miles an hour it would have been close on midnight before they arrived back or were picked up in carts and carried home.

Yet on their return there was a 'dinner as hearty as the breakfast', then more drinking of toasts with the dessert, then tea and coffee, then the ball at which Mr Pickwick kept 'perpetually dancing', then 'a glorious supper' and 'a good long sitting after it'. What did the Wardle staff think of all this? No doubt they were too drunk to care. But that prodigious feat of muscular and gastric endurance should not be confused with 'a regular Dickens Christmas' because that great day when it came was comparatively quiet. Christmas Eve at Dingley Dell was 'always an occasion for family games in the kitchen', with much kissing under the mistletoe, songs, and story-telling, and comparatively tranquil. Christmas Day had its 'substantial lunch with strong beer and cherry brandy' after church, and the skating- and sliding-party, after which Mr Pickwick, having broken the ice, had to be put to bed and thawed with bowls of punch. 'The jovial party' broke up next morning. The absorption of victuals and vintages on Christmas Day was almost a nibble and a sip compared with the gargantuan performance of the wedding-day.

There is no mention of Christmas presents at Dingley Dell. Mr Pickwick took with him as a contribution to the larder a codfish, which sounds rather dull, and a more appealing barrel of oysters. These got into the hands of the suddenly arriving Bob Sawyer, who was found 'a-openin' of 'em like steam'. It was not then thought necessary to spend anxious days in shopping, and selecting, in our catalogue language, 'suitable gifts for all ages'. The early Victorian Christmas did not involve copious presentation: the children had toys on the Christmas tree. The Boz picture of a Christmas dinner has a sparkling array of these, but it is not indicated that articles of clothing, books, calendars, and trinkets of all kinds had to be handed round to the adults, with considerable trepidation lest somebody had been left out.

The Christmas tree Dickens described as 'this German toy'. The notion that Queen Victoria's German Prince Consort planted the Christmas tree in our nurseries is inaccurate since Dickens had written thus of the tree's origin some years before the royal wedding. But undoubtedly German influence assisted its popularity and naturally the children welcomed larger and more heavily loaded trees as the cult of Christmas, with the stimulation of salesmanship, became steadily enlarged. The giving of presents had been in the past a New Year custom. Queen Elizabeth used to fill her already ample wardrobe by intimations to the members of her Court that new dresses were always acceptable when the day came. The response was tactfully and amply made. January presentations were customary for a very long time.

The history of Christmas or New Year giving is thus somewhat confused. The 'shopping spree' of our time, which packs the stores for weeks before the day, is a recent product of high wages and of times far less hard than those of the workers in Dickensian London and Coketown. Competitive commerce works on the normal desire to be generous and not to seem 'a snudge', a word partly superseded in our vocabulary by the invention of 'Scrooge'.

A very old kind of giving gave its title to Boxing Day, which is named after gratuities, not fists. On St Stephen's day, 26 December, the alms-boxes in the churches were opened and the contents distributed. There were boxes also in private houses and places of social gathering, small well-guarded chests with slots for coins. Samuel Pepys complained that 'boxing' had proved very expensive one Christmas, which indicates a good level of contribution. This kind of boxing had a long life and so established itself in the language that we still talk of a Christmas box when all we mean is a gift of money to those rendering regular service.

The Dickens Christmas, as was said, contained plenty of acting as well as story-telling round the fire. Improvising or having in mind a longish tale and not just an anecdote or funny story is a habit now almost vanished, like the readings aloud, especially of Dickens, which used to be a Christmas routine in a number of families. This custom was weakening before radio and television came in to smother it still further and perhaps altogether. But the lure of 'let's pretend' lingers on among the young and dressing up for a charade is a truly Dickensian exercise of invention. The early Christian Christmas absorbed the previous midwinter revels such as the Roman saturnalia, in which slaves had a temporary licence to masquerade as masters and enjoy a brief fling of freedom. The Church could not extinguish these rites, which sometimes became riotous, and the medieval Feast of Fools released, with clerical assent, a strong outburst of the saturnalian spirit.

The mummings took various forms. One was a general revel of rebellion against order with a Lord of Misrule, or in Scotland an Abbot of Unreason, chosen to be its sovereign in a world of topsy-turvy, where servants became lords, men dressed as women and women as men, and the skins and feathers of beasts and birds were worn in order to carry still further the escape from humdrum realities. The strength of tradition may be curiously seen in the British pantomime, one of whose long-surviving rules was the impersonation of the male hero or principal boy by a girl, the

'Now all common things become uncommon and enchanted to me'
—*Christmas Books*

playing of the comic old woman, or dame, by a man, and the careering of a nimble man in the coat of a dog or a cat or of two men presenting the fore and hind legs of a horse or cow. The Feast of Fools is not yet dead. The Reformation curbed but did not kill it. It could still kick its heels in the theatre of Dickens's time and in the antics of a Dickens nursery.

Another survival was the simply mimed folk play of the English villages, in which the death of winter and the revival of life in the New Year were symbolised by a dramatised story of a knight, usually St George, who fought and slew a dark enemy, usually a Turk. If the knight fell he was restored to life by a clever doctor. There had to be a conflict and a resurrection, as it were the battle of winter and spring, with the New Year triumphantly arising. If Dickens had been more of a countryman he would have cheered and rewarded the farm-land players (they expected their Christmas box) who went round from house to house with this mummery. There is a lively description of it in Thomas Hardy's *The Return of the Native*. But the Christmas play-going which Dickens knew was the visit to the urban pantomime. This was still based in his time on the amorous adventures and capers of Harlequin and Columbine, who were for a long time the chief characters but were ultimately driven into a last refuge at the end of the performance. This was known as the harlequinade and now has been dropped altogether. The player of the dame and other comedians with famous names have become the dominant attractions, highly paid and earning at the box-office their enormous salaries.

Pantomime, as Dickens had seen as a boy and remembered it with delight, was the direct descendant of the Italian comedy in which the fun was supplied by the foolish old man Pantaleone, who became Pantaloon and left his trousers as a legacy to our language, and by the clown, who made a fool of him. In his salute to a Christmas tree in *Christmas Stories* he recalled his boyish ecstasies:

> Comes swift to comfort me, the Pantomime—stupendous Phenomenon!—when clowns are shot from loaded mortars into the great chandelier, bright constellation that it is; when Harlequins, covered all over with scales of pure gold, twist and sparkle, like amazing fish; when Pantaloon (whom I deem it no irreverence to compare in my own mind to my grandfather) puts red-hot pokers in his pocket, and cries 'Here's somebody coming!' or taxes the Clown with petty larceny, by saying, 'Now, I sawed you do it!'; when Everything is capable, with the greatest ease, of being changed into Anything; and 'Nothing is, but thinking makes it so.'

There was also Astley's Circus but there were none of the Christmas plays for children that we have now. It is likely that Dickens at any year of his life would have been an enthusiastic addict of *Peter Pan*.

If Dickens were to see Christmas in his country as it is celebrated in the nineteen-sixties he would be astounded at the extent of it, the lengthy preparations, the vast expenditure, and the extent to which many of the shops depend on it for weeks of exceptional trade. With his own taste for letting money flow, for bounty of all kinds, and for a glittering spectacle, he would have approved the emptying of full purses by the crowds in the illumined streets and the groves of lamplit Christmas trees in public places as well as in private homes. He might wonder, however, whether beneath all the sumptuous display there were the motives and the purposes which had been at the heart of his impulsive religion and his use of the story to expose as well as to entertain. 'The broad beneficence and goodness that too many men have tried to tear to narrow shreds' are what he expressly demanded of the season along with the banquet and the social glass. 'A regular Dickens Christmas', were it true to Dickens as he knew it and not to the modern concept of 'a good time had by all' getting bigger and more costly as each Christmas comes round, would not be the kind of celebration which commerce has so largely taken over from the Church.

The Dickens Years

	The Life	*Some Events*
1812	Charles Dickens, son of John Dickens of the Navy Pay Office, born at Landport, Portsmouth, Feb. 7.	Britain at war with America. Peninsular War. French armies defeated in Spain at Badajoz and Salamanca. Napoleon invades Russia and is forced to retreat. Innovations in Britain include steam-power traction on colliery rail-tracks and the first steamboat passenger service. (This was on the Clyde.)
1813		Wellington completes the defeat of the French in the Spanish Peninsular War and enters France. George Stephenson constructs a steam locomotive which travels at six miles an hour.
1814	John Dickens transferred from Portsmouth to Somerset House and brings his family to London.	Napoleon defeated and sent to Elba. War with America ends. Steamboats on the Thames.
1815		Napoleon escapes from Elba and is finally defeated at Waterloo. Bourbons restored to the French throne. British Parliament passes a Corn Law to keep up the price of home-grown wheat.
1816		The end of the Napoleonic wars brings unemployment and bitter poverty. Rioting in the country and at Spa Fields in London.
1817	John Dickens transferred to Chatham and his family move again. The love of Kent with its coaches, shipping, and fruitful country-side implanted in the boy Charles an affection always ardently retained.	Great social unrest and repressive measures. Habeas Corpus suspended. Much new building in London. Waterloo Bridge opened.
1818		General Election brings another Tory Government but with reduced majority. Widespread demand for electoral reform.

	The Life	*Some Events*
1819		Queen Victoria born. Social discontent grows. Armed force used against a great meeting demanding reform, in St Peter's Fields, Manchester. The affray is called the Battle of Peterloo.
1820	Charles Dickens goes to the Academy of Mr Giles in Chatham, is well taught and encouraged, and becomes an avid reader.	
1821		Steamboats established between Dover and Calais.
1822	John Dickens goes back to London and the family settles in Camden Town, a district constantly reappearing in his son's books.	
1823	Hard times for the Dickens family owing to the father's feckless ways. Mrs Dickens tries to start a school and fails.	First naval steam-ship built at Deptford. Tariffs reduced and a policy of freer trade introduced by Huskisson.
1824	Hard times grow harder. Charles is sent to work in Warren's Blacking Factory near Charing Crosss. He hates the work and the humiliation of its necessity. John Dickens arrested for debt and sent to the Marshalsea Prison. Charles lodges near by in Lant Street, Southwark. A legacy rescues his father from the debtors' gaol and the family returns to Camden Town.	The Combination Act mitigates the restrictions on the forming of Trade Unions, but the common law of conspiracy is still applied and Trade Unionism is by no means secure. For example, Tolpuddle Martyrs (1834) are victimised for administering unlawful oaths, an excuse for crushing rural Trade Unionism.
1825–6	Charles Dickens, released from his factory work, becomes a pupil at Mr Jones's Classical and Commercial Academy in the Hampstead Road. Here he fairly well taught and shows his speed in learning.	The Stockton and Darlington Railway opened and stimulates further use of steam in land transport.
1827	Charles leaves school at Easter and becomes office-boy to a	Religious Tests for public office abolished.

	The Life	*Some Events*
1827	solicitor and then clerk to a firm of lawyers, Ellis and Blackmore, of Gray's Inn.	
1828	Continues as clerk and learns shorthand. Also learns much about the absurdities and cruelties of legal procedure which he was later to expose.	Catholic Emancipation at last admits Roman Catholics to nearly all positions in the State.
1829–31	Shorthand writer in the group of antiquated Courts known as Doctors' Commons. Falls in love, unrequited, with Maria Beadnell.	Continuing demands for higher agricultural wages lead to violence and violent repression. Accession of William IV and increasing demands for Parliamentary Reform. Cholera epidemic in London. Liverpool and Manchester railway opens. London gets omnibus service, three horses to each bus.
1832	Becomes a reporter for an evening paper, *The True Sun*, in the House of Commons in time for last stages of the Reform Bill and comes to despise 'the great dust-heap of Westminster'.	Reform Bill passed. Beginnings of national education made with a grant of only twenty thousand pounds from the Government.
1833–5	Makes his name as a speedy and accurate reporter of speeches in Parliament and at country political meetings. Begins to write other articles under the pseudonym of Boz.	Emancipation of slaves throughout the British Colonies. New Poor Law. Municipal Corporation Act ends some scandals of local government. Trade Unionism spreads. Factory Act secures a twelve-hour day and Factory Inspectors appointed. Such legislation hindered action of hostile employers.
1836	Dickens's first book, *Sketches by Boz*, published by Macrone and illustrated by Cruikshank. Chapman and Hall commission a volume of 'sporting misadventures' which become *The Pickwick Papers* appearing in serial form. A slow start for the sales, but the entry of Sam	Anti-Corn Law Association founded.

	The Life	*Some Events*
1836	Weller soon lifts them and makes Dickens famous at 24. He marries Catherine Hogarth.	
1837	Dickens settles in Doughty Street, Bloomsbury, in what is now Dickens House, open to the public. His first son, Charles, christened in St Pancras Church. Works on *Oliver Twist* and *Barnaby Rudge*.	Accession of Queen Victoria. Capital offences reduced to fifteen in number. Rapid development of railways. London to Birmingham line opened.
1838	Journeys to North Yorkshire to investigate the scandal of the 'Cheap Schools'. Discovers one which he described as Dotheboys Hall in *Nicholas Nickleby*, on which he starts work.	S.S. *Great Western* steams from Bristol to New York in sixteen days. People's Charter for universal suffrage (for men only) and annual Parliaments drawn up by Radicals. Chartism develops as an active movement.
1839	Publication of *Nicholas Nickleby* a huge success. Dickens now a public figure and a favourite public speaker. Works on *The Old Curiosity Shop*.	National Education grant raised to thirty thousand pounds. Penny Postage introduced.
1840	Moves to Devonshire Terrace.	Queen Victoria marries Prince Albert.
1841	Welcomed in Edinburgh and given the Freedom of the City.	
1842	Visits America. Warmly greeted and lionised, but is disappointed in 'The Land of Liberty' of which he had hoped too much. His outspoken book of *American Notes* infuriates all but his close friends and admirers in that country.	Female labour in mines forbidden by law. No boy under ten to work underground. Marshalsea Prison closed. Pentonville founded as a 'model prison' with solitary confinement as opposed to herding of prisoners. This proves a cruelty in many cases.
1843	*Martin Chuzzlewit* adds to that indignation. *A Christmas Carol* written.	Growth of middle-class prosperity leads to founding of several new schools called Public but essentially private.
1844–5	Travels in Italy and France. On return, devotes himself to amateur acting, discovering the histrionic capacities that were	Cheap Trains Act compels all lines to run one train each way daily at a penny a mile. Co-operative Movement foun-

	The Life	*Some Events*
1844–5	to be so profitable in his later readings of his work.	ded with first shop in Rochdale. Failure of potato crop leads to famine in Ireland. Wild gambling in railway shares. Factory Act eases conditions for women and children. The Corn Laws repealed.
1846	Becomes editor of *The Daily News* but soon resigns and returns to Europe.	
1847	Working on *Dombey & Son*.	Ten Hours Act limits the hours of women and children in textile factories to ten a day.
1848	Much travel, acting and speech-making.	Public Health Act appoints Board of Health to cope especially with the appalling conditions of sanitation. Chartist demonstration in London. Year of revolutions in Europe.
1849	*David Copperfield* appears in serial form. Dickens becomes half-owner and conductor of *Household Words*, thought by many to be an ideal magazine.	The revolutions in Europe cause alarm in Britain. Chartism fades away because of the violent methods threatened by its extreme supporters.
1850	First number of *Household Words*.	Pope establishes Roman Catholic hierarchy in England. Protestant fears of 'Romish' influence.
1851	Leaves Devonshire Terrace for Tavistock Place. Acts in Lytton's *Not So Bad As We Seem* before the Royal Family.	Sixth census shows population of United Kingdom to be just over 27,600,000.
1852	First parts of *Bleak House* appear.	Death of Wellington. Great public funeral.
1853	Completion of *Bleak House*. Travel in Italy.	
1854	Visits Lancashire and sees a strike and the sufferings of the workers. Writes *Hard Times*.	Crimean War begins.
1855	Working on *Little Dorrit* which begins to come out at the end of the year.	The inefficiency of military and civil administration exposed by the war keenly noted and satirised by Dickens.
1856	Stays in Paris. Buys Gad's Hill near Rochester which is to	End of Crimean War. Birth of Bernard Shaw, great

	The Life	*Some Events*
1856	remain his country house until his death.	admirer of Dickens.
1857	Acts in *The Frozen Deep*, a powerful drama by Wilkie Collins. Gives the first of his readings.	Indian Mutiny.
1858	Begins his affair with the actress Ellen Ternan. This breaks up his marriage.	Admission of Jews to Parliament without compulsion to take Christian oath.
1859	*A Tale of Two Cities* appears. Founds a new magazine, *All the Year Round.*	
1860–1	More public readings. Working on *Great Expectations.*	Death of Prince Consort. American Civil War.
1863–6	Busy with readings and speeches and starts work on *Our Mutual Friend.* Feels the strain and after being in a railway accident begins to lose the old confident vigour.	The American war causes great distress in Lancashire owing to failure of the cotton trade. Transatlantic telegraph cable laid and messages sent. American Civil War ends in 1865. Assassination of President Lincoln. End of slavery and foundation of Ku-Klux-Klan.
1867–8	Return visit to the United States. A bad reception is expected but a good one awaits him. The speeches and readings are triumphant, but exhausting.	Public Executions abolished.
1868–9	Visited by Longfellow at Gad's Hill. More readings and social occasions in Ireland and Scotland as well as England. Begins work on *Edwin Drood*, using the Rochester background.	
1870	Many public engagements despite ill-health. Received by Queen Victoria and kept standing for an hour and a half. A desperately tired man, he suffers a stroke at Gad's Hill and dies on June 9, leaving *Edwin Drood* unfinished. Buried in Westminster Abbey on June 14 amid widespread public mourning.	